Vampires of New England

by

Christopher Rondina

Photography by Berta Daniels
Original Illustrations by the Author

On
Cape Publications

www.oncapepublications.com

For Allan

*A fellow lover of life's dark shadows, mysterious tomes,
dusty corners, and lost secrets*

Acknowledgments

Vampires of New England is the fruition of a ten-year odyssey for me. My quest has taken me from lost graveyards to dusty library basements to archaeological digs and even to the crumbling fortress of Vlad Dracula in the mountains of Transylvania. How can I even *begin* to thank the legions of extraordinary people who have been a part of this crazy excursion into the dark corners of history?

First and foremost, thanks go to a trio of researchers without whom I could never have begun this journey: Michael Bell, Paul Sledzik, and Nick Bellantoni.

As ever, I owe a huge debt of gratitude to Berta Daniels, a wonderful photographer, true friend, and dauntless fellow adventurer.

Eternal gratitude to Jay Atwood for more reasons than I can ever relate.

To Josh Steele for being my rock during one of the most difficult times of my life.

To the borderless community of Babylon, my chosen family.

Deepest thanks are owed to both my Mother and my Father, who each gifted me in their own way with a fascination for monsters, mystery, and the unexplained.

Last, but far from least, in Memorium, Professor Raymond T. McNally (1931 – 2002). A wonderful friend, mentor, and scholar—"*Justus et pius.*"

Contents

Author's Note

It is the nature of legends that they will evolve from one telling to the next, often departing vastly from the original tale. In this volume, I've recounted these true vampire stories in my own words, while endeavoring to remain faithful to the actual events. I confess to using a bit of storyteller's license—adding dialogue and a handful of supporting characters, from village priests to wise old aunts—in an effort to paint a more vivid picture of these historic events. Such cinematic flourishes as twin puncture wounds and swooping bats seldom appear in the original accounts of New England vampires, and I do not employ them here. To highlight the historical basis of these legends, I have included transcripts from original newspaper accounts, scholarly papers, and articles that appeared at the time of these events.

Please note:
Some of the locations associated with the vampire legends are currently private property and are not accessible to casual visitors! When visiting any of the non-private locations—*especially graveyards*—please be respectful of your surroundings. These places are historical landmarks and are frequented by other people as well. The best motto to keep in mind is:

> "Take only photos; Leave only footprints"
> —Christopher Rondina, 2007

Introduction

Sunset. Trees and houses are visible only as shadowy silhouettes against the fading oranges of autumn dusk. Chill October air wraps itself around you, carrying with it the crisp odors of wood smoke and decay.

You walk quickly past the dark and silent houses as a flurry of dry leaves crackle and swirl about your feet. Nearby, an ancient cemetery lies carpeted with a thick blanket of scarlet and gold, its timeworn stones jutting from the earth like graying and broken teeth. Turning onto your own street, you see an inviting yellow glow coming from the windows of your home. Suddenly, you are startled by the whisper of wings just above your head. A large black bat darts by before vanishing into the shadows of the road ahead. Your heart races for a moment, then, laughing quietly to yourself, you continue on.

As you approach your home, you are surprised to notice that the door is open. You then realize that there are no longer any lights coming from within! From the darkness of the doorway, there suddenly appears an oddly pale man dressed in a long black coat. The stranger's lips glisten darkly in the fading light. You open your mouth to ask who he is, but before you can utter a word, he is gone! Within the house, all is silent. Overhead, the whisper of bat wings fades once more into the deepening night.

Do you believe in vampires? If so, you are not alone. No culture on Earth is without the legend of the *revenant* or "hungry ghost." Stories of the undead have terrified mankind since the earliest of times. Long before stories of vampires reached the shores of New England, tales of vengeful spirits and lost souls who preyed on the life forces of the unwary were commonplace in the mythology of most countries. In Eastern Europe, a common word for vampire was *Nosferatu*, a probable corruption of the word "*Necuratul*," meaning "un-decomposed" or "un-dead." Even today, the people of Romania's Transylvania region use garlic and other traditional methods to ward off the blood-drinking ghosts called *Strigoi*. The vampire is known throughout the world by many names: *Blutsauger* (Germany), *Penanggalan* (Maylaysia), *Jigar-Khor* (India), and *Vrykolakas* (Greece). In ancient China, a deceased body was carefully protected from exposure to moonlight in order to prevent its return as a *Kuang-Shi*. Even the practice of using headstones is believed to have started in Europe as a way to keep the dead in their graves, giving rise to the folk belief that a tilted gravestone marks the resting place of the living dead!

But what exactly *is* a vampire? Modern films like the series *Blade* and television shows such as *Blood Ties*, *Angel*, and *Buffy the Vampire Slayer* portray the vampire as essentially human-looking, only showing its true terrifying nature when about to attack. Most cinematic vampires have sharp canine teeth by which they feed, and many can transform into animals such as bats or wolves. Often aristocratic and wealthy, today's vampire is a seductive creature, easily attracting willing victims into a life of immortal splendor. But what of the vampires who came before the age of television and film?

Folklore defines a vampire as "a ghost or reanimated corpse which leaves its grave each night to feed upon the blood or life-force of the living." The actual word *vampire*, or *vampir*, is derived from a Slavic word meaning "blood drinker" and is believed to have entered the English language around 1732. In stark contrast to today's fiction, the vampires of ancient legend are more often ghastly than alluring, and are more likely to be found lurking in a moldering crypt than a lordly castle. Folkloric vampires come in a variety of forms, from spectral visitors to withered corpses or nightmarish monsters—hardly the sensual ideal so often portrayed on screen. Some of the better known aspects of vampire lore are accurate; aversion to garlic, wooden stakes, and infectious bites, for instance, all have their roots in early folklore. Many other generally accepted "rules" of vampirism, such as sharp canine teeth, burning in sunlight, or the existence of vampire "covens," are entirely the product of Gothic fiction from the 19th and 20th centuries.

The precise origins of the vampire are lost to history, but it is believed that the earliest such tales date back over 5,000 years to ancient civilizations such as Sumer and Ur. The genesis of the myth almost certainly stems from man's perceptions of the power and significance of blood. From very early times, humans became aware of the life-sustaining properties of blood.

Primitive man could endure a variety of injuries, including the loss of eyes, ears, or limbs, and still survive. By contrast, a relatively small wound that continued to bleed often led to death. Blood, by association, became regarded as the very essence of life itself.

In these early cultures, we also find references to angry gods with the power to *"cause the dead to rise up and to devour the living."* The concept of the sacred power of blood seems to have worked its way into many of these early religions. Blood sacrifice became a way to fend off the unwanted attentions of less benevolent gods. As ancient pantheons grew, some of these bloodthirsty "vampire-gods" were reduced to the stature of *"daemons"* or *"djinn"* (lesser gods) and, later still, to the diminutive role of demons and spirits. It is at this point that the image of the "traditional" vampire begins to take shape. The idea that the jealous dead might return to torment or steal the blood of the living must have been a logical extension of pre-existing notions about the relationships of blood and death.

The fully developed legend of the "blood-drinking ghost" rooted and flourished most strongly in the mountains of Eastern Europe, but tales of these *"Nosferatu"* have not remained confined to the Old World. In the years following the Revolutionary War, the people of Colonial New England began to experience outbreaks of an unknown wasting fever, which came to be known as "consumption." Medical science of the time seemed powerless to overcome the dreaded disease, leading people to the conclusion that the malady was a spiritual, rather than physical, condition. Faced with death after death from the mysterious fever, the frightened residents of dozens of rural communities from Rhode Island to Vermont fell to whispering the name of a nearly forgotten terror: *Vampire.*

New England has been called a vortex of "strange superstitions and twilight tales." Yankees perpetually walk a line between austere pragmatism in their daily lives and a kind of morbid pride in the ghosts and goblins that lurk in the darker recesses of local folklore. Even the most down-to-earth Yankee gets a devilish gleam in his eye when relating the details of an unsolved murder or haunted graveyard. This is never truer than in the autumn months. Fall in the Northeast simply cannot be surpassed. The trees seem to glow with fiery shades of scarlet, gold, and orange. The air is fragrant with wood smoke and apples, and nearly every porch boasts a fat pumpkin grinning like a harvest moon. It is in the autumn that you may chance upon the secret face of New England, hiding along crooked little roads so choked with vegetation that they might soon be overwhelmed or lurking behind hazy white farmhouses untouched by time. Rambling stone walls that once sheltered rebel colonists from Redcoat musket fire traverse the landscape, wrapping themselves around scattered tiny cemetery plots, where the less fortunate soldiers were soon to rest. Empty Colonial-era houses, with shadowy windows and banging shutters, slowly decay at the end of rutted dirt and gravel drives. The shadows in such places seem to hold secrets—*darker shadows* if you will—hiding among the graves and clapboards of old New England. If you doubt this, take a drive—or better still a walk—along one of these roads on a sunny October day. Keep in mind one thing as you go: *Shadows are always darkest in the daylight.*

Prologue

Anthropologist George Stetson wrote this treatise on the New England vampire phenomenon in the 19th century as the actual events were unfolding around him. Although at times a bit dry, it provides an excellent insight into the perspective of the scientific/medical community of the time when confronted by the legend of the vampire. It was originally published in *The American Anthropologist*, January 1896.

Note: This article contains some comments about "race" that are offensive by modern standards. Please keep in mind that the social climate of the late 1890s was much different than it is today.

The Animistic Vampire in New England

By George R. Stetson

The belief in the vampire and the whole family of demons has its origin in the animism, spiritism, or personification of the barbarian, who, unable to distinguish the objective from the subjective, ascribes good and evil influences and all natural phenomena to good and evil spirits. It has been remarked of this vampire belief that "it is, perhaps, the most formidable survival of demonic superstition now existing in the world."

Under the names of vampire, were-wolf, man-wolf, night-mare, night-demon — in the Illyrian tongue oupires, or leeches; in modern Greek broucolaques, and in our common tongue ghosts, each country having its own peculiar designation — the superstitious of the ancient and modern world, of Chaldea and Babylon, Persia, Egypt, and Syria, of Illyria, Poland, Turkey, Servia, Germany, England, Central Africa, New England, and the islands of the Malay and Polynesian archipelagoes, designate the spirits which leave the tomb, generally in the night, to torment the living.

The character, purpose, and manner of the vampire manifestations depend, like its designation, upon environment and the plane of culture. All primitive peoples have believed in the existence of good and evil spirits holding a middle place between men and gods. Calmet lays down in most explicit terms, as he was bound to do by the canons of his church, the doctrine of angels and demons as a matter of dogmatic theology.

The early Christians were possessed, or obsessed, by demons, and the so-called demoniacal possession of idiots, lunatics, and hysterical persons is still common in Japan, China, India, and Africa, and instances are noted in Western Europe, all yielding to the methods of Christian and pagan exorcists as practiced in New Testament times.

The Hebrew synonym of demon was serpent; the Greek, diabolus, a calumniator, or impure spirit. The Rabbins were divided in opinion, some believing they were entirely spiritual, others that they were corporeal, capable of generation and subject to death.

As before suggested, it was the general belief that the vampire is a spirit which leaves its dead body in the grave to visit and torment the living. The modern Greeks are

persuaded that the bodies of the excomm
putrefy in their tombs, but appear in the
day, and that to encounter them is dangerou

Instances are cited by Calmet, in Christi
excommunicated persons visibly arising f1
and leaving the churches when the deacon commanded the
excommunicated and those who did not partake of the
communion to retire. The same writer states that "it was an
opinion widely circulated in Germany that certain dead ate
in their tombs and devoured all they could find around
them, including their own flesh, accompanied by a certain
piercing shriek and a sound of munching and groaning."

A German author has thought it worth while to write a
work entitled "De Masticatione mortuorum in tumulis." In
many parts of England a person who is ill is said to be
"wisht" or "overlooked." The superstition of the "evil eye"
originated and exists in the same degree of culture; the evil
eye "which kills snakes, scares wolves, hatches ostrich eggs,
and breeds leprosy." The Polynesians believed that the
vampires were the departed souls, which quitted the grave,
and grave idols, to creep by night into the houses and
devour the heart and entrails of the sleepers, who afterward
died.[1] The Karems tell of the Kephu, which devours the
souls of men who die. The Mintira of the Malay Peninsula
have their water demon, who sucks blood from men's toes
and thumbs.

"The first theory of the vampire superstitions," remarks
Tyler[2], "is that the soul of the living man, often a sorcerer,
leaves its proper body asleep and goes forth, perhaps in
visible form of a straw or a fluff of down, slips through the
keyhole, and attacks a living victim. Some say these Mauri
come by night to men, sit upon their breasts, and suck their
blood, while others think children alone are attacked, while
to men they are nightmares.

The second theory is that the soul of a dead man goes out from its buried body and sucks the blood of living men; the victim becomes thin, languid, bloodless, and, falling into a rapid decline, dies."

The belief in the Obi of Jamaica and the Vaudoux or Vodun of the West African coast, Jamaica and Haiti is essentially the same as that of the vampire, and its worship and superstitions, which in Africa include child-murder, still survive in these parts, as well as in several districts of this country.

In New England the vampire superstition is unknown by its proper name. It is there believed that consumption is not a physical but a spiritual disease, obsession, or visitation; that as long as the body of a dead consumptive relative has blood in its heart it is proof that an occult influence steals from it for death and is at work draining the blood of the living into the heart of the dead and causing his rapid decline. It is a common belief in primitives of low culture that disease is caused by the revengeful spirits of man or other animals.

Russian superstition supposes nine sisters who plague mankind with fever. They lie chained up in caverns, and when let loose pounce upon man without pity.[3] As in the financial and political, the psychologic world has its periods of exultation and depression, of confidence and alarm. In the eighteenth century a vampire panic beginning in Servia and Hungary spread thence into northern and western Europe, acquiring its new life and impetus from the horrors attending the prevalence of the plague and other distressing epidemics in an age of great public moral depravity and illiteracy. Calmet, a learned Benedictine monk and abbé of Sénones, seized this opportunity to write a popular treatise on the vampire, which in a short time passed through many editions. It was my good fortune not long since to find in the Boston Athenaeum library an original copy of his work. Its title page reads as follows: "Traité sur les apparitions des esprits et sur les vampires ou les revenans de Hongrie, de Moravie, etc. Par le R. P. Dom Augustine Calmet, abbé de Sénones. Nouvelle edition, revisée, corrigie, at augmentie par l'auteur, avec une lettre de Mons le Marquis Maffei, sur le magie. A Paris; Chez debure l'aine quay des Augustins à l'image S. Paul. MDCCLI. Avec approb et priv du roi." Calmet was born in Lorraine, near Commercy, in 1672, and his chief works were a commentary and history of the Bible. He died as the abbé de Sénones, in the department of the Vosges.

This curious treatise has evidently proved a mine of wealth to all modern encyclopedists and demonologists. It impresses one as the work of a man whose mental convictions do not entirely conform to the traditions and dogmas of his church, and his style at times appears somewhat apologetic. Calmet declares his belief to be that the vampires of Europe and the broucolaques of Greece are the excommunicated, which the grave rejects. They are the dead of a longer or shorter time who leave their tombs to torment the living, sucking their blood and announcing their appearance by rattling of doors and windows. The name vampire, or d'oupires, signifies in the Slavonic tongue a bloodsucker. He formulates the three theories then existing as to the cause of these appearances:

First: That the persons were buried alive and naturally leave their tombs.

Second: That they are dead, but that by God's permission or particular command they return to their bodies for a time, as when they are exhumed their bodies are found entire, the blood red and fluid, and their members soft and pliable.

Third: That it is the devil who makes these apparitions appear and by their means causes all the evil done to men and animals.

In some places the spectre appears as in the flesh, walks, talks, infests villages, ill uses both men and beasts, sucks the blood of their near relations, makes them ill, and finally causes their death.

The late Monsieur de Vassimont, counselor of the chamber of the courts of Bar, was informed by public report in Moravia that it was common enough in that country to see men who had died some time before "present themselves at a party and sit down to table with persons of their acquaintance without saying a word and nodding to one of the party, the one indicated would infallibly die some days after."[4]

About 1735 on the frontier of Hungary a dead person appeared after ten years' burial and caused the death of his father. In 1730 in Turkish Servia it was believed that those who had been passive vampires during life became active after death; in Russia, that the vampire does not stop his unwelcome visits at a single member of a family, but extends his visits to the last member, which is the Rhode Island belief.

The captain of grenadiers in the Regiment of Monsieur le Baron Trenck, cited by Calmet, declares "that it is only in their family and among their own relations that the vampires delight in destroying their own species."

The inhabitants of the island of Chio do not answer unless called twice, being persuaded that the broucolaques do not call but once and when so called the vampire disappears, and the person called dies in a few days. The classic writers from Socrates to Shakespeare and from Shakespeare to our own time have recognized the superstition.

Mr. Conway quotes from the legend of Ishtar descending to Hades to seek some beloved one. She threatens if the door is not opened—

> "I will raise the dead to be devourers of the living;
> Upon the living shall the dead prey."[5]

Singularly, in his discourse on modern superstitions De Quincey, to whom crude superstitions clung and who had faith in dreams as portents, does not allude to the vampire; but his contemporary, Lord Byron, in his lines on the opening of the royal tomb at Windsor, recognizes this belief in the transformation of the dead:

> "Justice and death have mixed their dust in vain,
> Each royal vampire wakes to life again."

William of Malmsbury says that "in England they believed that the wicked came back after death by the will of the devil," and it was not an unusual belief that those whose death had been caused in this manner, at their death pursued the same evil calling. Naturally under such an uncomfortable and inconvenient infliction some avenue of escape must, if possible, be found. It was first necessary to locate the vampire. If on opening the grave of a "suspect" the body was found to be of a rose color, the beard, hair and nails renewed, and the veins filled, the evidence of its being the abode of a vampire was conclusive. A voyager in the Levant in the seventeenth century is quoted as relating that excommunicated person was exhumed and the body found full, healthy, and well disposed and the veins filled with the blood the vampire had taken from the living. In a certain Turkish village, of forty persons exhumed seventeen gave evidence of vampirism. In Hungary, one dead thirty years was found in a natural state. In 1727 the bodies of five religieuse were discovered in a tomb near the hospital of Quebec, that had been buried twenty years, covered with flesh and suffused with blood.[6]

The methods of relief from or disposition of the vampire's dwelling place are not numerous, but extremely sanguinary and ghastly. In Servia a relief is found in eating of the earth of his grave and rubbing the person with his blood. This prescription, was, however, valueless if after forty days the body was exhumed and all the evidences of an arch-vampire were not found. A more common and almost universal method of relief, especially in the Turkish provinces and in the Greek islands, was to burn the body and scatter the ashes to the winds. Some old writers are of the opinion that the souls of the dead cannot be quiet until the entire body has been consumed. Exceptions are noted in the Levant, where the body is cut in pieces and boiled in wine, and where, according to Voltaire, the heart is torn out and burned.

In Hungary and Servia, to destroy the demon it was considered necessary to exhume the body, insert in the heart and other parts of the defunct, or pierce it through with a sharp instrument, as in the case of suicides, upon which it utters a dreadful cry, as if alive; it is then decapitated and the body burned. In New England the body is exhumed, the heart burned, and the ashes scattered. The discovery of the vampire's resting-place was itself an art.

In Hungary and in Russia they choose a boy young enough to be certain that he is innocent of any impurity, put him on the back of a horse which has never stumbled and is absolutely black, and make him ride over all the graves in

the cemetery. The grave over which the horse refuse
is reputed to be that of a vampire.

Gilbert Stuart, the distinguished American painter, when
asked by a London friend where he was born, replied: "Six
miles from Pottawoone, ten miles from Poppasquash, four
miles from Conanicut, and not far from the spot where the
famous battle with the warlike Pequots was fought." In
plainer language, Stuart was born in the old snuff mill
belonging to his father and Dr. Moffat, at the head of the
Petaquamscott pond, six miles from Newport, across the
bay, and about the same distance from Narragansett Pier,
in the state of Rhode Island.

By some mysterious survival, occult transmission, or
remarkable atavism, this region, including within its
radius the towns of Exeter, Foster, Kingstown, East
Greenwich, and others, with their scattered hamlets and
more pretentious villages, is distinguished by the prevalence
of this remarkable superstition— a survival of the days of
Sardanapalus, of Nebuchadnezzar, and of New Testament
history in the closing years of what we are pleased to call
the enlightened nineteenth century. It is an extraordinary
instance of a barbaric superstition outcropping in and
coexisting with a high general culture, of which Max
Müller and others have spoken, and which is not so
uncommon, if rarely so extremely aggravated, crude, and
painful.

The region referred to, where agriculture is in a depressed
condition and abandoned farms are numerous, is the
tramping ground of the book agent, the chromo-peddler, the
patent-medicine man and the home of the erotic and
neurotic modern novel. The social isolation away from the
larger villages is as complete as a century and a half ago,
when the boy Gilbert Stuart tramped the woods, fished the
streams, and was developing and absorbing his artistic
inspirations, while the agricultural and economic
conditions are very much worse.[7]

Farmhouses deserted and ruinous are frequent, and the once productive lands, neglected and overgrown with scrubby oak, speak forcefully and mournfully of the migration of the youthful farmers from country to town. In short, the region furnishes an object-lesson in the decline of wealth consequent upon the prevalence of a too common heresy in the district that land will take care of itself, or that it can be robbed from generation to generation without injury, and suggests the almost criminal neglect of the conservators of public education to give instruction to our farming youth in a more scientific and more practical agriculture. It has well been said by a banker of well-known name in an agricultural district in the midlands of England that "the depression of agriculture is a depression of brains." Naturally, in such isolated conditions the superstitions of a much lower culture have maintained their place and are likely to keep it and perpetuate it, despite the church, the public school, and the weekly newspaper. Here Cotton Mather, Justice Sewall, and the host of medical, clerical and lay believers in the uncanny superstitions of bygone centuries could still hold high carnival.

The first visit in this farming community of native-born New Englanders was made to ------, a small seashore village possessing a summer hotel and a few cottages of summer residents not far from Newport— that Mecca of wealth, fashion, and nineteenth-century culture. The ------ family is among its well-to-do and most intelligent inhabitants. One member of this family had some years since lost children by consumption, and by common report claimed to have saved those surviving by exhumation and cremation of the dead.

In the same village resides Mr. ------, an intelligent man, by trade a mason, who is a living witness of the superstition and of the efficacy of the treatment of the dead which it

18

prescribes. He informed me that he had lost two brothers by consumption. Upon the attack of the second brother his father was advised by Mr. ------, the head of the family before mentioned, to take up the first body and burn its heart, but the brother attacked objected to the sacrilege and in consequence subsequently died. When he was attacked by the disease in his turn, ------'s advice prevailed, and the body of the brother last dead was exhumed, and "living" blood being found in the heart and in circulation, it was cremated, and the sufferer began immediately to mend and stood before me a hale, hearty, and vigorous man of fifty years. When questioned as to his understanding of the miraculous influence, he could suggest nothing and did not recognize the superstition even by name. He remembered that the doctors did not believe in its efficacy, but he and many others did. His father saw the brother's body and the arterial blood. The attitude of several other persons in regard to the practice was agnostic, either from fear of public opinion or other reasons, and their replies to my inquiries were in the same temper of mind as that of the blind man in the Gospel of Saint John (9:25), who did not dare to express his belief, but "answered and said, Whether he was a sinner or no, I know not; one thing I know, that whereas I was blind, now I see."

At ------, a small isolated village of scattered houses in a farming population, distant fifteen or twenty miles from Newport and eight or ten from Stuart's birthplace, there have been made within fifty years a half dozen or more exhumations. The most recent was made within two years, in the family of ------. The mother and four children had already succumbed to consumption, and the child most recently deceased (within six months) was, in obedience to the superstition, exhumed and the heart burned. Dr. ------, who made the autopsy, stated that he found the body in the usual condition after an interment of that length of time. I learned that others of the family have since died, and one is now very low with the dreaded disease. The doctor remarked that he consented to the autopsy only after the pressing solicitation of the surviving children, who were patients of his, the father first objecting, but finally, under continued pressure, yielding. Dr. ------ declares the superstition to be prevalent in all the isolated districts of southern Rhode Island, and that many instances of its survival can be found in the large centers of population. In the village now being considered known exhumations have been made in five families, and in two adjoining villages in two families. In 1875 an instance was reported in Chicago, and in a New York journal of recent date I read the following: "At Peukuhl, a small village in Prussia, a farmer died last March. Since then one of his sons has been sickly, and believing that the dead man would not rest until he had drawn to himself the nine surviving members of the family, the sickly son, armed with a spade, exhumed his father and cut off his head." It does not by any means absolutely follow that this barbarous superstition has a stronger hold in Rhode Island than in any other part of the country. Peculiar conditions have caused its manifestation and survival there, and similar ones are likely to produce it elsewhere. The singular feature is that it should appear and flourish in a native population which from its infancy has had the ordinary New England educational advantages; in a State having a larger population to the square mile than any in the Union, and in an environment of remarkable literacy and culture when compared to some other sections of the country. It is perhaps fortunate that the isolation of which this is probably the product, an isolation common in sparsely settled regions, where thought stagnates and insanity and superstition are prevalent, has produced nothing worse.

In neighboring Connecticut, within a few miles of its university town of New Haven, there are rural farming populations, fairly prosperous, of average intelligence, and furnished with churches and schools, which have made themselves notorious by murder, suicides, and numerous instances of melancholia and insanity.

Other abundant evidence is at hand pointing to the conclusion that the vampire superstition still retains its hold in its original habitat — an illustration of the remarkable tenacity and continuity of a superstition through centuries of intellectual progress from a lower to a higher culture, and of the impotency of the latter to entirely eradicate from itself the traditional beliefs, customs, habits, observances, and impressions of the former.

It is apparent that our increased and increasing culture, our appreciation of the principles of natural, mental, and moral philosophy and knowledge of natural laws has no complete correlation in the decline of primitive and crude superstitions or increased control of the emotions or the imagination, and that to force a higher culture upon a lower, or to metamorphose or to perfectly control its emotional nature through education of the intellect, is equally impossible. The two cultures may, however, coexist, intermingling and in a limited degree absorbing from and retroacting favorably or unfavorably upon each other— trifling aberrations in the inexorable law which binds each to its own place.

The most enlightened and philosophic have, either apparent or secreted in their innermost consciousness, superstitious weaknesses — negative, involuntary, more or less barbaric, and under greater or lesser control in correspondence with their education, their present environment, and the degree of their development — in the control of the imagination and emotions. These in various degrees predominate over the understanding where reason is silent or its authority weakens.

Sónya Kovalévsky (1850–1890), one of the most brilliant mathematicians of the century, who obtained the Prix-

Bordin from the French academy, "the greatest scientific honor ever gained by a woman," "whose love for mathematical and psychological problems amounted to a passion," and whose intellect would accept no proposition incapable of a mathematical demonstration, all her life maintained a firm belief in apparitions and in dreams as portents. She was so influenced by disagreeable dreams and the apparition of a demon as to be for some time thereafter obviously depressed and low-spirited. A well-known and highly cultured American mathematician recently said to me that his servant had seven years ago nailed a horseshoe over a house door, and that he had never had the courage to remove it. There is in the Chemnitzer-Rocken Philosophie, cited by Grimm, a register of eleven or twelve hundred crude superstitions surviving in highly educated Germany. Buckle declared that "superstition was the curse of Scotland," and in this regard neither Germany nor Scotland are singular.

Of the origin of this superstition in Rhode Island or in other parts of the United States we are ignorant; it is in all probability an exotic like ourselves, originating in the mythographic period of the Aryan and Semitic peoples, although legends and superstitions of a somewhat similar character may be found among the American Indians.

The Ojibwas have, it is said, a legend of a ghostly man-eater. Mr. Mooney, in a personal note, says he has not met with any close parallel of the vampire myth among the tribes with which he is familiar. The Cherokees have, however, something analogous. There are in that tribe quite a number of old witches and wizards who thrive and fatten upon the livers of murdered victims. When some one is dangerously sick these witches gather invisibly about his bedside and torment him, even lifting him up and dashing him down again upon the ground until life is extinct. After he is buried they dig up his body and take out the liver to feast upon. They thus lengthen their own lives by as many

days as they have taken from his. In this wa
very aged, which renders them objects of s
not, therefore, well to grow old among the
discovered and recognized during the feast, v
again visible, they die within seven days. I l
experience of a case in which a reputed medic
left to die alone because his friends were afraid to come into
the house on account of the presence of invisible witches.

Jacob Grimm[8] defines superstition as a persistence of
individual men in views which the common sense or culture
of the majority has caused them to abandon, a definition
which, while within its limits sufficiently accurate, does
not recognize or take account of the subtle, universal,
ineradicable fear of or reverence for the supernatural, the
mysterious, and unknown.

De Quincey has more comprehensively remarked that
"superstition or sympathy with the invisible is the great test
of man's nature as an earthly combining with a celestial. In
superstition is the possibility of religion, and though
superstition is often injurious, degrading and demoralizing,
it is so, not as a form of corruption or degradation, but as a
form of non-development."

In reviewing these cases of psychologic pre-Raphaelitism
they seem, from an economic point of view, to form one of
the strongest as well as the weirdest arguments in favor of a
general cremation of the dead that it is possible to present.
They also remind us of the boutade of the *Saturday Review*,
"that to be really Medieval, one should have no body; to be
really modern, one should have no soul;" and it will be well
to remember that if we do not quite accept these demonic
apparitions we shall subject ourselves to the criticism of the
modern mystic, Dr. Carl du Prel, who thus speaks of those
who deny the miraculousness of stigmatization: "For these
gentleman the bounds of possibility coincide with the limits

of their niggardly horizon; that which they cannot grasp either does not exist or is only the work of illusion and deception."

Chapter 1

1793, Rachel Burton, VT

At its core, the vampire is a creature of supreme will, resisting the pull of death by grasping at the life that surrounds it. Eerily reminiscent of Edgar Allan Poe's " Ligiea " is the story of Rachel Burton, among the earliest incidents of vampirism yet unearthed in New England.

Early in 1790, Captain Isaac Burton lost his wife of less than a year to the wasting fever called "consumption." Characterized by the coughing of blood and a slow, lingering decline, the fever had destroyed Rachel's body but never dampened her will to live. In her final hours, she seemed to grow almost stronger as the fiery determination to continue burned in her eyes. At the end, Rachel had gripped her husband's hand with unnatural strength as she whispered hoarsely to him before breathing her last, *"I won't leave! I'll be with you—always…"*

Rachel's passing deeply affected Captain Burton, and for a time he remained secluded in the large home he had built for him and his wife. Eventually, however, duty compelled Isaac to face the world once more. Almost exactly one year after Rachel's death, the Captain took a new bride. Hulda Powell became Hulda Burton, and Isaac's life began anew. Sadly, a peaceful existence was not fated for the husband or his new bride.

A few months into the marriage, the robust Hulda began to show signs of the strange wasting fever. Dread washed over Isaac as he recognized the symptoms of the illness that had claimed his beloved Rachel. Though he knew it would prove ultimately futile, Captain Burton threw the weight of his considerable wealth into summoning doctors from around the region in desperate hope of saving his second wife.

The attending physicians were unable to stem the progress of Hulda's decline. Soon, she was confined to her bed, even as Rachel had been before her. Mrs. Burtons's nearby relations began to take turns looking after her when Isaac was unavailable, applying cool, dampened cloths to her fevered brow and encouraging her to drink broth to keep up her strength. It was following such a vigil by an elderly aunt that Isaac was offered a chilling explanation for his wife's illness. The old woman was blunt in her assessment, claiming that a 'wicked spirit' was drawing the blood from Hulda's body. Isaac was stunned by the woman's wild theory, but his horror was doubled when she pressed the issue.

"It's the one who went a'fore that's to blame," the old woman spat. "The one who can't rest for want of the life she's lost!"

Isaac needed no clarification of the woman's meaning. He vividly remembered the willful determination in his first wife's eyes as she had proclaimed, *"I'll be with you—always..."* before slipping into death.

Hulda's aunt paused at the door as she was leaving. "It's got to be burnin'. That's the only way to stop the heart beatin' sure."

The following sunrise found Isaac gathered with a small group of family and friends at the grave of Rachel Burton. Two hired men were in the process of unearthing Rachel's coffin from the cold and frosty ground. By the time the box was pulled free of the earth, the assembled group was chilled to the marrow by the late winter damp. A close family friend, Selectman Timothy Mead, had agreed to preside at the exhumation, allowing Isaac to be minimally involved in the act.

The casket, once opened, revealed a bloated corpse, barely recognizable as Rachel Burton. "Gorged on the blood of its victim! *Look*! See the stains about the mouth!" Hulda's aged aunt pointed accusingly at the still figure in the box.

Clearly hoping to end the grisly affair as expediently as possible, Selectman Mead spoke up. "It is confirmed then." Clearing his throat and speaking in a firm voice, he continued, "Having duly concluded that the life of Mrs. Hulda Burton is jeopardized by unnatural attentions cast upon her by the former wife of Captain Isaac Burton, it is judged that the aforementioned abomination be destroyed in the prescribed manner."

A sizable crowd had gathered at the blacksmith's forge to witness the finale of the bizarre event. The heart, liver, and lungs of Rachel Burton had been removed and were now cast into the searing coals of the forge. The stench that rose from the burning organs was almost overwhelming, and several onlookers later reported seeing the apparition of a terrible beast writhing in the greasy column of black smoke that billowed from the coals.

Despite the completion of the grim remedy, Hulda Burton did not survive. Family members surmised that she was too weakened by the ordeal to recover from the ravages of the fever, but they were quick to point out that the malady did not pass along to another in the ensuing years. Isaac Burton lived to a ripe age, but never again remarried.

Chapter 2

1796, Abigail Staples, RI

On a quiet road in Northern Cumberland sits a small, neglected cemetery dating back to the Revolutionary War. Broken stones and accumulated layers of dead leaves are the only memory remaining of this branch of the Staples family.

Beneath the soil of the ancient plot, however, may reside the unquiet bones of Abigail Staples, who died over two hundred years ago at the age of twenty-three. Sadly for the family, Abigail's early death does not seem to have been the end of her story. In the months following her demise, the members of the Cumberland Town Council were petitioned with an unusual request:

From Cumberland Town Council records, 1796

At a town Council held at Cumberland in the County of Providence, being specially called and held on the eighth day of February 1796.

Present members:
> Mr. John Lapham
> Mr. Jason Newell
> Capt. Benjamin S. Westcott
> Mr. Benjamin Singly

Mr. Stephen Staples of Cumberland appeared before this council and prayed that he might have liberty granted unto him to dig up the body of his daughter Abigail Staples, late of Cumberland, single woman, deceased, in order to try an experiment on Lavinia Chace, wife of Stephen Chace, which said Lavinia was sister to said Abigail, deceased.

Which being duly considered it is voted and resolved that the said Stephen Staples have liberty to dig up the body of the said Abigail, deceased, and after trying the experiment as aforesaid that he bury the body of the said Abigail in a decent manner.

Voted that this Council be dissolved.

Witness, Mr. Jonathan Carpenter, Council Clerk.

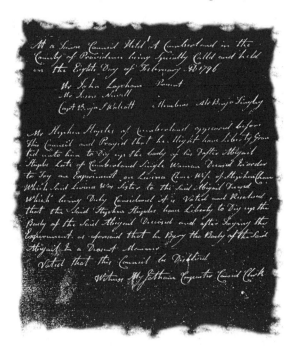

Original Cumberland Town Council meeting notes on the exhumation of Abigail Staples, 1796

Shortly after the death of her sister Abigail, Lavinia Chace fell prey to "consumption," whereupon her life seemed to be draining slowly from her body, leaving her weaker and paler each day. In Lavinia's fevered dreams, she was tormented and smothered each night by a shadowy figure that perched upon her chest, crushing her with its weight and then drawing out her breath as though feeding upon it. Lavinia confessed the dreams to her husband, Stephen, who reassured her that the nightmares would pass.

One morning as Stephen was beginning to wake, Lavinia sat bolt upright in bed and cried *"Abigail!"* before falling once more into a fitful sleep. Much disturbed by the strange episode, Stephen went that evening to the home of his father-in-law, Stephen Staples, to tell him of Lavinia's outburst.

Mr. Staples sat at the kitchen table warming his hands on a mug of hot wine. He listened patiently to the young man's account of his wife's behavior, staring silently into the guttering flame of the lamp that rested upon the table.

"I'm not sure what to think sir," the younger man continued, "but it *is* odd, is it not?"

"Odd—yes." Staples's words were slow, considered. "I'm not much given to ideas of witchery and spooks, Stephen."

"Nor I, sir, and yet…if such things exist, if there's a chance?"

Staples rubbed a hand across his face. He looked weary, older than his considerable years. "This is no simple matter, boy. If we're to pursue this sort of madness, then we'll need to have the support of the rightful authorities."

"Do you think that wise, sir? If they refuse…"

"If they refuse, then we obey their judgment! The alternative is the gallows for both of us!"

Stephen bit back any further comment he might have considered. The call had been made. Now it would fall to the town Elders to decide.

"A *vampyre?*"

A rumble of low comments moved through the assembled council members. Ben Westcott, a portly man who had been decorated during the War for Independence, spoke up. "Mr. Staples, we extend our condolences on the recent loss of your daughter Abigail. We sympathize also with the condition of your daughter Lavinia and pray for her swift recovery."

Council Chair John Lapham continued. "The unusual matter of which you speak is somewhat outside our area of expertise, I'm afraid. Frankly, we are somewhat unsettled to hear a sensible man such as yourself putting forth such a notion."

Undaunted by the council's skepticism, Mr. Staples pressed his point. "Surely you don't mean to suggest that our Sunday worship is an act of folly Mr. Lapham? Yet only this week past were we counseled by our good pastor on the wiles and dangers of the Devil and his demons."

The councilman appeared momentarily taken aback by Staple's argument, allowing Stephen Chace to take up the thread. "Would it not be wiser, sirs, to grant license for this endeavor in the sake of the community's good? If it's for naught, then no great harm done, yet if it be true, and allowed to fester..." The younger man trailed off, as though unwilling to speculate on the consequences of inaction.

Mr. Lapham held his hand up to silence the two petitioners. "Of course I mean no disrespect for our pastor *or* his words—though you might do well to regard them more *philosophically* in the future." He sat back in his chair and regarded the two gentlemen before him.

"Very well," said Lapham with an exaggerated sigh, leaning forward to take up a quill and paper. "Your request is granted, though it is against the better conscience of this council," he continued, as he began to draft the order. "See that your daughter is re-interred with full respect at the conclusion of this affair—and I charge you also to see that this 'experiment' is conducted with a *minimum* of spectacle."

The hillside cemetery was away from common view on the Staples's property, but, mindful of the council's request, the men made their way there in the late hours of night just the same. Of Abigail's condition when the grave was opened, no record exists, nor can we be certain of the events that followed. Local legend says that what the two men saw when they opened the coffin so terrified young Stephen Chace that he fled the darkened graveyard ranting like a madman. The elder Mr. Staples never spoke of what he witnessed, but from that night on he was a changed man, with hollow haunted eyes and terrible nightmares. As for Lavinia Chace, her fate is unknown. No gravestone marks her burial place, and no further record of her seems to exist—as if she was swallowed by the darkness of that dreadful night, never to be seen again.

The Staples family burial ground

Chapter 3

1799, Sarah Tillinghast, RI

In the years following the American Revolution, there lived in the South County area of Rhode Island a farmer named Stuckley Tillinghast. Stuckley was often called by the nickname of "Snuffy"—a reference to his home-sewn coat, which was said to be the color of tobacco snuff. Snuffy was known to be a good-natured man and not prey to bouts of fancy or superstition.

Selling his apples and peaches throughout the state, Stuckley managed to provide decently for his family. Honour—Stuckley's wife—maintained a busy but well-ordered household, caring for their many children. All but the youngest of the flock helped in the orchards or tended to the few livestock, which were kept mostly for the family's needs. Many years passed happily enough for the Tillinghast clan, as the older children grew up and married and new little ones were brought into the world. By 1790, Stukley and Honour had eight daughters and six sons, the youngest having arrived in early October.

The harvest season of 1799 began like many before it, with a ripening crop of apples just waiting to be picked. Stuckley liked to remark that a breath of air on the Tillinghast farm was "like breathing cider." Honour would often chide him that after thirty-five years of working the farm, he would smell cider if he was cleaning the hog pen. Soon, the lives of the family and farmhands were immersed in the task of bringing in the crop.

One chilly night after a long day in the orchard, Snuffy woke in a panic from a dream. After Honour had calmed him, he related the nightmare that had unnerved him so:

> I was working among the trees when I heard our daughter Sarah calling to me. As I turned to look for her, a cold wind picked up, blowing the leaves all around me, so that I was nearly blinded. When the wind died down, I looked to find Sarah, but she was nowhere in sight. I turned back to the trees to continue working and saw that the leaves had all turned brown, and the fruit was rotting on the branches. A smell of decay washed over me, and I was nearly ill. Stepping back I saw that fully half of the orchard was dead!

Honour reassured him that it was only a nightmare, but his sleep that night was not a restful one.

In the following nights, Tillinghast's sleep was broken by the dream again and again. Disturbed by the grim omen, Snuffy sought the advice of a local pastor, Benjamin Northup. No help was forthcoming from that source, however. The clergyman simply told him that worry over the harvest was invading his rest and assured him that as soon as the crops were in the trouble would cease. Snuffy politely took leave of the pastor and went home, scarcely comforted by Northup's words.

Despite his fears, harvest season did indeed pass without incident, and soon enough the family began to settle in for the coming winter. With the crops safely in, the dream receded to the back of Snuffy's mind.

Sarah, who had just turned nineteen this season, was quiet and kept to herself. When not helping in the house or fields, she preferred to do her stitchwork or read her mother's old books. This being so, it was not at first very alarming when she began to stay in her room for hours at a time, coming down only to take meals with the family. Soon it became apparent, however, that Sarah was ill. As days grew into weeks, it was clear to the family that she was not long for this world. Sarah died and was laid to rest in the family plot. The doctor's diagnosis was "consumption."

A few weeks after Sarah's passing, James, the youngest of the Tillinghast boys, came down to the kitchen early one morning. Honour was already up, and had a coffee pot boiling on the cast-iron stove. Still rubbing the sleep from his eyes, James complained to his mother of a pain in his chest. Honour looked knowingly at the boy.

"And I suppose you've been into your papa's green apples again, eh?" Honour asked as she brushed a stray lock of hair from her son's forehead. The boy shook his head vigorously.

"Honest no, mama, it hurts here," James pointed at the wooden button on his shirt that rested above his heart, "where Sarah touched me." The mention of Sarah's name brought Mrs. Tillinghast an unexpected wave of melancholy, which seemed out of place on the mild spring day. When she answered the boy, her voice was gentle.

"James, Sarah is gone now," Honour put her arms around the boy and gently hugged him. "I dream about her too sometimes. We all miss her very much."

James hugged tightly to his mother and began to cry. As he tried to choke back his tears, Honor could hear an unhealthy rattling in his breathing.

Honour put the boy immediately to bed and saw to it that he took plenty of hot broth and vinegar. She piled him high with blankets and shut the windows to keep out the bad night air, but all in vain. Over the next few weeks, James grew very weak, fading much as his sister had before him. Looking at him, his mother couldn't help but recall his strange words: "...*where Sarah touched me.*"

In the end, James joined his sister in the ground.

Young Andris, aged fourteen, was next to grow ill, and after her, Ruth, the next eldest to Sarah. Both girls shared a strange complaint—that their sister Sarah was visiting their room by night.

Andris told her mother that she was awoken from sleep by a sound like bells heard from far away.

> I went to open the window so I might hear it more clearly. It seemed such a very pretty sound. As I turned the latch, I noticed Sarah standing in the yard below. She called to me—and then she was in the room, though I don't recall how she got there.

Ruth told of a similar visitation: "Sarah came and stood by the bed and leaned over me. I couldn't see her face, but I knew by her voice that it was Sarah. She said that she missed me, and that she was very cold, and needed to be warm."

At this, Honour felt a chill move along her spir
hugged me then, mama, but she squeezed so tight
catch my breath."

Both girls were gone in a matter of months.

The Tillinghasts began to fear that some blight had been called down upon their family. Honour told Snuffy of the eerie visitations the children had spoken of. "Nightmares," Honour insisted, but her voice was uncertain. "The children were only having nightmares, weren't they?"

A creeping dread stole upon Snuffy as he began to suspect what meaning his own terrible dreams had foreshadowed. Returning to Reverend Northup in town, Snuffy told the man of his suspicions. Once again, the pastor tried to assure him that things would right themselves in God's time and that to pray was his best hope.

Time passed, and the Tillinghasts prayed with tears on their cheeks and sour hearts, day after day, while the family was consumed by the wasting sickness.

The strange visitations by Sarah did not remain within the walls of the Tillinghast farm. Hannah was among the older of the Tillinghast daughters. Nearly twenty-six, she and her husband lived a few miles away in West Greenwich. Hannah visited often and had lately been helping to tend to her sick siblings. Soon she, too, began to have visions of Sarah.

Honour became pale as her daughter spoke of the dreams. She pleaded with Hannah. "You mustn't come to visit anymore! Not while this—this *Evil* is haunting us!"

"Mama, don't be foolish! The strain of these last few months is too much for you to bear alone. Papa can't ignore the farm, and you *need* my help."

Honour argued, but Hannah would not hear of it. She insisted that the strength of their family would overcome any misfortune. Hannah hugged her mother tightly. "We are stronger than any nightmares."

Hannah succumbed to the sickness in the late spring of the following year. On the night following Hannah's burial, Honour's sleep was fitful. In her dreams she was suffocating from the stale air of the bedroom, and she went to open the window for a breath of cool air. As she stood relishing the breeze on her face, a wave of fetid air seemed to enter the room. Honour wrinkled her nose in disgust and reached to close the panes, when she felt a presence in the room. She turned to see her lovely daughter Sarah standing in the center of the tiny bedroom, looking longingly at her.

"Mama?" Sarah held out her open arms to Honour. "Mama, it's so lonely, so cold—won't you come with me?" With tears streaming down her face, Honour walked over to her daughter and was enfolded in her arms.

One warm evening, there came a polite knock at the door of the farmhouse. Jeremiah Dandridge, an acquaintance of the family, had come to offer condolences on Hannah's recent passing. Honour invited him in and set the teapot on for their guest. Snuffy chatted with the gentleman for a while, noting that Dandridge seemed somewhat nervous. After a little while, he seemed to gather his nerve and told Snuffy of the similarity between Sarah's passing and the tragedy of a family in nearby Richmond, some years earlier. According to the stories, Jeremiah said, the dead were thought to have reached out from the grave and tormented the dreams of the family, causing several of them to die. Snuffy listened to the man's story, his face fixed like a granite mask. Tillinghast stood and asked his friend if they could finish the conversation outside. Honour watched for a little while from the kitchen window as the two men spoke quietly on the porch. When Dandridge had gone, Snuffy returned to the house.

Tillinghast walked upstairs to the room where he found Honour keeping vigil over his seventeen-year-old son, Ezra, who lay in bed shaking with fever. He told his wife what he had heard and what would need to be done. Honour clutched a fist to her mouth in horror at his words, but Snuffy's resolve hardened as he looked upon his eldest son stricken in this way. He set about making preparations for the task ahead.

Tillinghast and two of his strongest farmhands loaded a cart with rope, shovels, a mattock, and a flask of oil. Hitching up a horse, they set off for the small burial ground nearby, where six of his children had so recently been interred. Hanging at his side in a leather sheath, Snuffy carried a large hunting knife.

The men spent the following hours digging the crude wooden coffins of Snuffy's children from the earth. From last buried to first, each box was pulled free of its grave. Some of the children had been in the ground for many months and were far along in their state of decay. All this Tillinghast took in with hard eyes, having been blunted by pain and grief in these last months.

Late afternoon approached as at last the men came to pull Sarah's box from the ground. She had been in the earth for almost six months. Removing the lid, Tillinghast nearly lost the composure he'd fought so hard to maintain on this most terrible of days. He took a deep breath and looked upon his daughter.

Sarah lay as if resting, her body looking flushed and vital in the amber glow of the late day. Her eyes were open, staring glassily at the darkening sky, yet seeing nothing. One of the farmhands, Caleb, dropped to his knees and clasped his hands together while muttering ill-remembered prayers from his youth. Ben, the other, stepped back from the box as though the girl might spring at him. He averted his eyes from the maddening sight.

Snuffy removed the large knife from his belt and, wiping tears away with his sleeve, spoke to Caleb.

"Go fetch the oil from the cart."

Caleb still knelt near the grave, whispering prayers. When the man did not respond, Tillinghast barked the order again, his control nearly breaking under the strain. Caleb stumbled to his feet and ran to the cart, trying to ignore the terrible sound of Snuffy's blade as the man crouched over the pale form in the coffin and began his gruesome task. Caleb grabbed the flask and came back to the graveside. Tillinghast stood and tossed something to the ground near the feet of the other farmhand. Ben gasped and ran to the gate of the cemetery, where he stood shaking.

Snuffy held out a dark-stained hand for the flask of oil, then produced flint and tinder from his coat pocket. He poured the oil onto the small reddish lump that lay there in the grass. Striking a flame to the tinder, Tillinghast watched as his daughter's heart burnt to ash.

Young Ezra's condition was too advanced for the remedy to take effect, and he died soon after. Honor recovered completely, however, and brought two more children into the Tillinghast household. All of the remaining Tillinghast children would go on to outlive their parents. In the end, Snuffy Tillinghast's dream had come to pass. Of his fourteen children, seven had died—exactly half of his "orchard."

To this day, the Tillinghast family burial ground wooded spot near the former site of Snuffy's orchards, just off Victory Highway in the township of Exeter, Rhode Island. It is easily missed by the casual passerby, but within its walls are perhaps fifteen to twenty evident stone markers. Several other markers are hidden in the brush or fallen over and are difficult to spot. The gravestone of "Snuffy" Stuckley Tillinghast is small and squat, with only the crudely carved letters S. T. to identify it as his. Nearby lies his wife, Honour, who died in 1831 at the age of eighty-seven. A few yards from her parents, among the resting places of the siblings she is accused of preying upon, lies the unmarked grave of Sarah Tillinghast—and there her bones sleep for eternity.

Chapter 4

1827, Nancy Young, RI

Spring 1806

Captain Levi Young assisted his wife, Anna, down from the seat of their small carriage. Cradled in the nook of one arm, Anna held a tiny infant, mercifully quiet after the tiring journey from their Connecticut house to this rural Rhode Island farm.

"*Home*, Anna. What do think?" Levi's infectious smile brightened his face as he took in the rustic-looking house and its sprawling acres.

"Are you certain we are in Rhode Island?" Anna asked, "I thought it was supposed to be a small state!" Her own smile conveyed her delight at the sight of their new home.

Dispatching Anna to the house, Levi wandered over to where Elija, his one slave, sat atop the cart, laden with the family's worldly possessions. Elija was not a young man, having belonged to Levi's father before him. Levi considered Elija to be a member of the family, allowing him to take meals with them and giving him a room in the main house.

"It's a fine place, Mister Levi, mighty fine." Elija's deep voice was thoughtful. "A good place for the boy to grow in." With a huff, the old man climbed from the seat of the cart and the two of them set about the long task of unloading.

Autumn of the following year brought the first crop of the new farm. The harvest was modest—native corn, potatoes, onions, and a few bushels of beans. In midsummer, Anna had discovered a thicket of wild blackberries near the rear of the property, and so the family bolstered their income a bit with Anna's excellent preserves, which fetched a good price in the nearby capital city of Providence.

October brought another gift to the house as well—an infant girl, Nancy. In the years that followed, the Young farm continued to grow, as did the Young household. In time, Anna bore Levi eight children, and the house rang with the sounds of a prosperous family. Elija had grown too old to work the fields, but with the older boys in the family, Levi had no call to hire more servants. The old slave passed his last years in the comfort of a cottage on the farm and was eventually laid to rest in the family plot.

Years passed, and Nancy grew into a fine woman. She was smart, with a quick wit and an even temperament. By the age of nineteen, Nancy was managing most of the accounting and ledger work of her father's farm.

Sadly, the bountiful times were coming to an end for the Young family. Early in 1827, disaster struck. Nancy contracted what at first seemed to be a severe cold. She was bedridden while her sister Almira struggled to take over the farm's bookkeeping. Soon however, the fever from which Nancy suffered overtook her, and she began to weaken. On the sixth day of April, 1827, Nancy died of "Galloping Consumption."

A few months after Nancy's death, Almira became ill with a similar condition. The progress of the affliction was slow, but it eventually sapped her strength and confined her to bed. Levi arranged for the best doctor in the region, but he was powerless to stop the strange fever from ravaging the poor girl.

One morning, Levi went to Almira's room to bring her a mug of tea. He tapped lightly on the door before entering to see the girl smiling. "Papa, I think I'm getting well!" Levi forced a smile for his daughter, who looked very frail and weak as she sat propped up against the pillows of her bed. Almira continued, "Last night I dreamt that Nancy came to visit me!"

"Oh?"

"She was so bright papa, like an angel! She told me that the pain would go away soon, and then she held my hand, and I forgot all about being sick for a while." Almira's bright face clouded for a moment as her body was wracked with coughs.

Levi looked at the pale form of his daughter wasting away before him. A dark fancy occurred to him as Almira continued to describe her deceased sister's appearance in the dream.

"Papa?" Levi realized that Almira was looking at him, expecting a response. He reached over and brushed a wisp of hair from the young girl's eyes. "Yes, little squirrel, I'm sure you'll be well soon." He kissed her forehead and stood. "Sleep for now."

Levi admitted to himself that he was unnerved by Almira's dreams. He began to wonder if conventional medicinal remedies would not provide the answer to his dilemma. Local history was peppered with strange tales—talk of unquiet spirits who lived beyond the grace of God by drawing forth the blood of the living. Loathsome as the thought was, he had to consider that Nancy might indeed be reaching out from the grave. Requesting a meeting of the town fathers, he confessed his suspicions. The elders concluded that Levi's household was indeed being tormented by such a demon, and it must be driven out. The assumption was that the restless spirit would be found lingering in the family cemetery, residing within the coffin of the firstborn daughter.

A small collection of townsfolk accompanied Levi and the other members of the Young family to the newly walled-off burial ground near the back of the Young farm. The single slate grave marker within the walls looked like a penitent child standing in the corner of a schoolhouse after a scolding. The somber group filed quietly through the gate to stand before Nancy's solitary grave.

One of the eldest present was a gaunt, white-bearded man, Nathan "Doc" Lennox. Old Nate wasn't truly a doctor, but he was knowledgeable in some strange ways and was often called upon in cases like this one. Doc gestured to two of the more burly young men who'd come along. "You boys go and fetch up some wood an' brush, an' start pilin' it up like you was goin' to build one hell of a bonfire."

The older of the two, Jim Attwood, spoke up. "Where, Doc? Things are kinda dry—we don't want no fire catchin' into the fields or woods!"

"Right there then, up to the other wall." The old man indicated the far corner of the little plot. "No reason the ashes can't stay with the dead where they b'long." Jim nodded and the two men clambered over the low stone wall and went to work collecting wood.

Throughout this exchange, Levi Young had sat immobile on the stones at the edge of the small plot. He held his hands clasped in front of him and seemed to stare vacantly at his daughter's cold stone. The other members of the Young family stood around him and watched as several of the townsmen bent to the task of unearthing Nancy's coffin.

"No."

For a moment everyone froze. Levi was getting to his feet. In the slanting rays of the late afternoon sun, his eyes were the color of iron. "I should be the one to begin. It is my burden, and I will not ask any of you to do what I would not."

Levi reached out and took a shovel from the hands of Ben McClure. Ben was a pleasant-looking fellow only a little older than Nancy would have been if she had lived. Ben and Nancy had known each other for most of their lives. Levi knew that Ben had harbored some affection for his eldest daughter, and he supposed this must be hard for the boy. He gave Ben's shoulder a light squeeze. "Thank you, Ben." Looking up at the assembled crowd he continued. "Thank you all."

By sunset, the coffin containing the shrouded white figure of Nancy Young lay atop a pyre of old farm wood, branches, and dry brush. Levi did not speak as he set a torch to the base of the wooden mound. The fire caught fast, and soon the pyre was awash with crimson flame, spiraling up into the blackness of the descending night.

Doc Lennox had advised the members of the Young family to stand around the fire so that the vapors from the blaze could cleanse them of any contamination by the evil that had claimed Nancy. Braving the searing heat, the family joined hands and allowed the smoke to wash over them. The others present maintained a distance from the flaming bier, standing outside the wall of the cemetery. By morning, the exhausted family and onlookers had returned to their homes. Little more than ash remained of Nancy Young.

Sadly, the unusual remedy employed by the members of the Young family does not appear to have helped. The already stricken Almira died within a year of the exhumation of Nancy. As the years passed, four more of Levi and Anna's children died of consumption. None of the other children were ever exhumed.

Hidden within a stand of trees in the most rural area of the town of Foster, Rhode Island, is the forgotten burial ground of the Young family. Most of the stone markers remain standing, hidden among the weeds and bushes that overgrow the remote little plot. The dates on the tombstones speak plainly of the creeping death that overtook the family of Nancy Young more than a century and a half ago.

Chapter 5

1834, The Corwin Family, VT

The following 1966 newspaper article—which includes the complete text of an 1890 article—was authored by Rockwell Stephens.

"The Vampire's Heart"
Mischief in the Mountains

In the fall of 1890 there appeared on the first page of Woodstock's weekly newspaper, *The Vermont Standard*, a story that might well have come out of the seventeenth instead of the 19th century. On page 1 of the issue of October 9, under the simple arresting headline:

Vampirism in Woodstock

was the following, which we give verbatim:

The following remarkable story is reprinted here as given in the *Boston transcript.* A further elucidation of the matter is furnished below.

Even in New England curious and interesting material may be found among older people descended from the English colonial settlers. About five years ago an old lady told me that, 50 years before our conversation, the heart of a man was burned on Woodstock Green, Vermont. The man had died of consumption six months before and the body was buried in the ground. A brother of the deceased fell ill soon after and in a short time it appeared that he too, had consumption; when this became known the family decided at once to disinter the body of the dead man to examine his heart. They did so, and found the heart undecayed, and containing liquid blood. Then they reintered the body, took the heart to the middle of Woodstock green, where they built a fire under an iron pot, in which they placed the heart and burned it to ashes.

The old lady who told me this was living in Woodstock at the time, and said she saw the disinterment and burning with her own eyes.

We may as well help the old lady's recollections in this matter, and fill in with further details what she has left incomplete. To be particular in dates, the incident happened about the middle of June, 1830. The name of the family concerned was Corwin, and they were near relatives of the celebrated Thomas Corwin, sometime senator in Congress from Ohio, well known for his wit and attractiveness as an orator. The body disinterred was buried in the Cushing Cemetery. With regard to the cause of the illness that had seized the brother of the deceased, there was a general consensus of opinion among all the physicians of the time practicing in Woodstock. These embraced the honored names of Dr. Joseph A. Gallup, Dr. Burnwell, Dr. John D. Powers, Dr. David Palmer and Dr. Willard who recently died in New York, not to mention other members of the profession at that time residing in Woodstock, and held in the high regard at home and abroad. These all advised the disinterment as above described, all being clearly of the opinion that this was a case of assured vampirism. Only there was a slight controversy between Drs. Gallup and Powers as to the exact time that the brother of the deceased was taken with consumption. Dr. Gallup asserted that the vampire began

54

his work before the brother died. Dr. Powers was positively sure that it was directly after.

The boiling of the pot on Woodstock green, spoken of by the old lady, was attended by a large concourse of people. The ceremonies were conducted by the selectmen, and attended by some of the prominent citizens of the village then residing on the common. It will suffice to name the Honorable Norman Williams, Gen. Lyman Mower, General Justus Durdick, B. F. Mower, Walter Palmer, Esq., Woodward R. Fitch, old men of renown, sound-minded fathers among the community, and discrete careful men. The old lady has forgotten to state what was done with the pot and its ghastly collection of dust after the ceremonies were over. A hole ten feet square and fifteen feet deep was dug right in the center of the park where the fire had been built. The pot with the ashes was placed in the bottom, and then on top of that was laid a block of solid granite weighing seven tons, cut out of Knox Ledge. The hole was then filled up with dirt, the blood of a Bullock was sprinkled on the fresh earth, and the fathers then felt that vampirism was extinguished forever in Woodstock. Eight or ten years after these events some curious minded persons made excavations in the park to see if by chance anything might be found of the pot. They dug down 15 feet, but found nothing. Rock, pot, ashes and all had disappeared. They heard a roaring noise, however, as of some great conflagration, going on in the bowels of the earth, and a smell of sulfur began to fill the cavity, whereupon, in some alarm they hurried to the surface, filled up the whole again, and went their way. It is reported that considerable disturbance took place on the surface of the ground for several days. Where the hole had been dug some rumblings and shaking of the earth, and some smoke was emitted.

What to make of this grisly tale? Witchcraft in the 19th century? Preposterous! An exorcism such as this in a community as prosperous as Woodstock in the mid-1830s? Did none of the "sound-minded fathers among the community, discrete careful men" make a protest at a rite of medieval sorcery in a town boasting many doctors, a young medical college, and more than the usual number of men of outstanding talent and industry?

In fairness to the "prominent citizens" and to the doctors, we may examine this fantastic story in the light of its time. Superstition, though no longer a guiding principle, had by no means been scotched by either church or science. The eighteenth century is heavily documented with nostrums and practices to ward off evil— natural and supernatural. The last witch had been hanged in Salem long before, but like folk music, the mythology lingered on for another century or more.

As late as 1750 a treatise on vampirism written in Europe in 1734 was translated into English and widely read as an aftermath of the period when all Europe was filled with reports of the exploits of vampires. They were supposed to be the souls of dead men which quit their buried bodies by night to suck the blood of living persons. Hence when the vampire's grave is opened, his body is found to be fresh and rosy from the blood consumed.

Such progress as medicine had made by our year 1830 had done but little to enlighten the rural population. Despite an unavailing voice here and there, the period saw a flowering of nostrums, many liberally laced with 100-proof alcohol, which were an accepted part of every home medicine chest for another generation at least.

Could the medical men of the town in fact have concurred in their verdict of "an assured case of vampirism"? One can speculate that they felt they were dealing, as in undoubtedly many other cases, with *force majeur*, that protest would only deepen the suspicions against which they constantly worked.

Who were these medical men and what was their training?
Dr. Joseph A. Gallup, one of the founders of the
Woodstock, Vermont, medical college, was considered the
leading physician of eastern Vermont. He was one of the
few then practicing who, as a member of the Dartmouth
College medical school's first graduating class, had any
formal training. The author of several books, including an
appendix on consumption, he was "highly praised for his
experimental knowledge." He was president of the medical
college on its establishment in 1826 and gave all the lectures
for several years.

Evidently a man of firm and outspoken opinion, he became
the leader of a faction which apparently created a
controversy sufficiently widespread to merit comment in a
Rhode Island doctor's essay on medical delusions. Dr.
Gallup's party of New England medical men contended that
the general character of the diseases of the time were
inflammatory, and hence bloodletting was his "Grand
Remedy." The opposition contended that this general
character was essentially opposite, or "asthenic," and relied
largely on opium and brandy in treating diseases.

Castigating the "asthenics," Gallup is quoted: "It is probable
that for 40 years past, opium and its preparations have done
seven times the injury that they have rendered benefit on
the great scale of the world." The Opposition: "The lancet is
a weapon that annually slays more than the sword," and
"the King of Great Britain loses more subjects every year by
this means than the battle and campaign of Waterloo cost
him with all its glories."

Like many another of this time, Dr. Gallup eventually had
an eye for business, and we find him the joint proprietor of
a drugstore in the town. A regular feature of the advertising
columns of Woodstock's *Weekly Observer* was nearly half a
column extolling "essence of life— a valuable medicine
discovered by Dr. Jona Moore, a very worthy physician of
Putney, Vermont, [that] has stood unrivaled amidst the

downfall of hundreds of medicines which have been offered to the public as specifics for the same diseases (as indicated on the label) and has been the means of snatching thousands from the jaws of death.

"This essence answers a valuable purpose in almost every case of debility, and there are few if any diseases which do not arise from that source. It may be given to either sex and at any period if weakness prevails, the composition being entirely derived from the vegetable kingdom."

This modest statement is followed by heartfelt endorsement by ministers of the gospel in Putney, Dummerston, Westminster and Brattleborough. The advertisement concludes with the lines: "Dr. Moore's essence of life — for sale, wholesale and retail at the store of Gallup and Taylor — Woodstock."

Of the other doctors listed as concurring in the judgment of vampirism, Dr. John D. Powers was perhaps the more typical of his time. He had learned his medicine from his father, Stephen Powers, who in turn got his training from the older doctors in Massachusetts between 1750 and 1755, and who moved Woodstock with the first families in 1774. Dr. John is assumed by some local historians to have ousted Dr. Gallup as head of the Vermont medical college — which was obliged to close in '61 — and was said to be "rather old-fashioned." It is perhaps significant that he disagreed with Dr. Gallup on whether the victim of our vampire fell ill before or after the malignant creature's death.

Dr. John Burnell, whom the author of our story identifies as "Burnwell" came to Woodstock in 1809, boarded for a time with Dr. Gallup, and planned to take Dr. Gallup's practice, as he was busy with the store, but Burnell evidently was disappointed in this hope. He nevertheless made his reputation in the community by his success in a "lung fever" epidemic in 1813, and was noted as one of the earliest practitioners of vaccination. An advertisement in the *Observer* of 1820 informs that "Kine Pock v̶ effective in preventing smallpox" and that "Dr. Bur vaccinate any who call for it." Dana's *History of W* says, "Dr. Burnell always felt the greatest interest in the advancement of medical science as opposed to quackery and empiricism," and asserts he "had a truly scientific mind."

We can only speculate whether one of the town doctors conducted the dissection of the vampire's heart, said to have been found "undecayed and containing liquid blood." The dissection would've been welcomed by one of the medical students, whose supply of cadavers was so limited that grave robbing had become a cause of contemporary outcry. The practice was evidently so frequent that the medical school had been forced to make a public promise "not use any human body which might be disinterred here about."

The question of "liquid blood" raises a nice point. It is in the tradition of true vampirism that the creature's heart contains blood drawn from its victims. Our tale avers that this vampire's death occurred some six months before the exorcism. What does pathology say about the stated presence of liquid blood existing in a body six months after death?

"Impossible — strictly speaking," say all three of Woodstock practicing physicians today. "But," asks the layman, probing "might there be fluid of a sort, perhaps discolored, which a person, predisposed to find blood, would think of as blood?" Two votes for "yes — maybe."

The list of "prominent citizens of the village then residing on the common" is perfectly valid. It would also be in keeping that the ceremonies be conducted by the selectmen, though these, three in number as of today, were not named. Town records identified them as John D. Pratt, Jason Kendall, and Nathan T. Churchill.

Did any of these leave a journal that might throw light on the occasion? If so, it is still buried in some attic. But this line of inquiry at last produced virtually unimpeachable evidence of the continuing existence of the key superstition on which the story is based.

In the stacks of the Norman William Public library on Woodstock Green — and incidentally on the site of the onetime home of the honorable Norman Williams listed as an Observer — is a folder containing some 70 typed pages, labeled "Memoirs of Daniel Ransom." There are short biographical outlines of various members of the Ransom family, one of the very earliest to settle in town and distinguished for a succession of outstanding men in every generation. The following is copied from page 20:

Frederick Ransom, the second son of my father and mother, was born in South Woodstock, Vermont, June 16, 1797, and died of consumption Feb. 14, 1817, at the age of about 20. He had a good education and was a member of Dartmouth College at the time of his death. My remembrance of him is quite limited, as I was only three years old at the time of his death, and I date my remembrance of anything to a visit of Dr. Frost to Frederick in his sickness, keeping shy of the doctor, fearing he would freeze me.

It has been related to me that there was a tendency in our family to consumption, and that I, who now in 1894 am over 80 years old, would die with it before I was 30. It seems that father shared somewhat in the idea of hereditary diseases and withal had some superstition, for it was said that if the heart of one of the family who died in consumption was taken out and burned, others would be free from it. And father, having some faith in the remedy, had the heart of Frederick taken out after he had been buried, and it was burned in Capt. Pearson's blacksmith forge. However, it did not prove a remedy, for mother, sister, and two brothers died with that disease afterward.

Mother did indeed die, of consumption (as tuberculosis was then called) in 1821, followed by sister in 1828 and other brothers in 1830 and 1832.

Here, in any event, is a case of exorcism only 13 years prior to our story. How many others took place in those years when consumption, diagnosed as such or simply labeled "fever," was a major killer — when doctors were generally mistrusted, and medical science was just beginning to emerge from the dark ages?

There is little doubt that the connection between a burned heart and consumption was a widespread belief springing from medieval times and persisting well into the 19th century. In his *Doctors of the American Frontier* Richard Dunlop says, "The fried heart of a rattlesnake could be eaten to cure consumption along most of the frontier as it moved westward."

The ritualistic concept of blood is practically a contemporary survival. The sprinkling of blood or ashes of the sacrificial animal has been an accepted rite of purification from medieval times. Hence in embellishing our tale, the author naturally felt it appropriate that when the hole in which our vampire's heart burned was filled, "the blood of a Bullock was sprinkled on the fresh earth."

So how stands our cast for belief or disbelief in this grisly tale? The case fits the times, the cast of characters is established, but what of our accused — one Corwin, male, torn from his grave in the Nathan Cushing Cemetery in the town of Woodstock on that June day of 1830?

The Cemetery is there, above the north bank of the Ottauquechee stream, flanked on the South and West by town roads and the East and North by the pastures and mowings of a modern dairy farm. But among the headstones dating to the early days of the town, none bears the name Corwin. Nor does the careful script on the pages own register of births and death record a Corwin. name is not found in census or land records of Woodstock or the adjacent Pomfret—which also used Cushing plots. So, speculation ends, as it often must, with a question mark. We may take this tale or leave it, or file it as a testimonial of the tragic helplessness of families of those times when faced with the mysteries of sickness and death.

As stated, there is no sign today of a Corwin family burial in the Nathan Cushing Cemetery, though visitors to Woodstock, VT, may enjoy a stroll among the historical stones nonetheless. Regarding that sinister iron pot which is said to rest beneath Woodstock Green? I can only caution the unwise traveler to heed the lesson of those foolhardy men who tried once before to uncover that dark artifact.

Chapter 6

Circa 1850, J. B., "The Griswold Vampire," CT

The town of Griswold, CT, is the sort of place easily missed by most people. Quiet and rural, Griswold consists mostly of older farms and homes, alongside a number of small, unassuming businesses. The people there are pleasant, though as reserved as one expects Yankees to be. It would certainly come as a surprise to most passers-through, headed for Hartford or other points, that the soil of Griswold has been hiding a vampire for nearly 150 years. In this chapter, Paul S. Sledzik and Nicholas Bellantoni present the evidence.

Bioarcheological and Biocultural Evidence for New England Vampire Folk Belief

By Paul S. Sledzik and Nicholas Bellantoni (1994)

Many cultures have developed folk beliefs to explain the natural phenomena associated with death and disease (Aries, 1981). The folk belief in vampires, found in many cultures, incorporates interpretations of death and disease. The vampire image found in contemporary Euroamerican culture is based solely on Bram Stoker's *Dracula*, an image that varies significantly from historic European and American vampiric folk beliefs. Eighteenth century European peasants believed that the appearance of the vampire in the grave (i.e., bloated chest, long fingernails, and blood draining from the mouth) meant that the vampire was draining life from the living. We now know these changes to be the result of postmortem decomposition (Barber, 1988; Mann et al., 1990; Micozzi, 1992). Further, the high number of deaths resulting from disease epidemics were also blamed on vampires. To stop the epidemic, vampires were sought out and "killed" by various methods (Perkowski, 1989). The term vampirism has also entered the psychiatric literature to explain pathologic behaviors similar to those of the mythical vampire, particularly ingestion of blood and necrophagic and cannibalistic activities (McCully, 1964; Prins, 1984; Vanden Bergh and Kelly, 1964). The clinical manifestation of erythropoietic protoporphyria, also known as Gunther's Disease, and its variants have also been cited as an explanation for the vampire belief (Prins, 1985). This autosomal dominant disorder causes increased excretion of protoporphyrin and results in redness of the eyes and skin, a receding of the upper lip, and cracking of the skin when exposed to sunlight.

American vampire folk beliefs, which were particularly strong in 19th century New England, contained some European features. The New England folklore is consistent in its incorporation of tuberculosis and examination of the body of the vampire for putative signs of life. Following the death of a family member from consumption (i.e., tuberculosis), other family members began to show the signs of tuberculosis infection. According to the New England folk belief, the "wasting away" of these family members was attributed to the recently deceased consumptive, who returned from the dead as a vampire to drain the life from the surviving relatives. The apotropaic remedy used

kill the vampire was to exhume the body of the supposed vampire and, if the body was un-decomposed, remove and burn the blood-filled heart or the entire body.

It stands to reason that the bioarcheological evidence of the vampire belief should be located in 19th century New England cemeteries. This report presents the analysis and interpretation of the grave of a supposed vampire from 19th century Connecticut, emphasizing the effect of the vampire folk belief on the bioarcheological record. This report also shows the importance of using historic documentation in the interpretation of skeletal information (Owsley, 1990; Sledzik and Moore-Jansen, 1991).

Skeletal Evidence
The Walton Cemetery, Griswold, Connecticut, an abandoned 18th–19th century Euroamerican rural farm family burial ground, was discovered eroding out of an operating, privately owned sand and gravel business in November 1990. Unfortunately, the instability of the sand and gravel knoll precluded in situ preservation and necessitated archeological removal of all remaining burials. The skeletal remains of 29 individuals (15 subadults, 6 adult males, and 8 adult females) were excavated in the course of 1 year. Documentary evidence in land deeds indicated that the Walton family, who had emigrated to Griswold in 1690, had utilized the knoll as a family burial ground by the 1750s.

The pathological conditions observed in the burials from the Walton Cemetery reflect lives of physical labor, including osteoarthritis and an unhealed femoral neck fracture in an elderly female. One case of particularly heavy dental calculus was observed.

The complete skeleton of a 50- to 55-year-old male interred in a stone-lined grave is of particular interest for this report. Two observations regarding this skeleton are of note: 1) the postmortem rearrangement of the skeletal remains, and 2) paleopathological evidence of a probable pulmonary tuberculosis infection.

Upon opening the grave, the skull and femora were found in a "skull and crossbones" orientation on top of the ribs and vertebrae, which were also found in disarray. On the coffin lid, an arrangement of tacks spelled the initials "JB-55", presumably the initials and age at death of this individual.

Pathological conditions evident in this skeleton included healed fractures and active infectious processes. Healed fractures were observed on the lateral half of the right clavicle (with a bony callus extending to the scapula), the right eighth rib, and the left second rib. Mild osteoarthritis was seen in most large joints and most lower vertebrae. Some lower vertebrae also exhibited Schmorl's nodes. The articular surface of the left femoral medial condyle presented an area of crenulated bone 30-mm in diameter, probably traumatic in origin. Focal lytic activity had

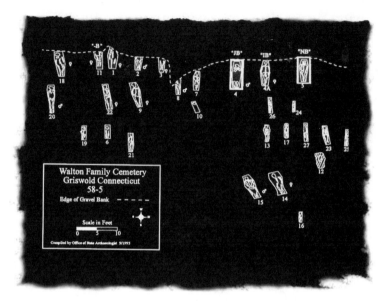

The forgotten cemetery where the bones of the
Griswold Vampire were unearthed

destroyed an area of bone approximately 40 mm
in diameter at the articulations of the left
metatarsals and cuneiforms. Periostitis was
present on the distal half of the left tibia and the
distal two thirds of the left fibula. Periostatic
lesions of the left second, third, and fourth ribs
were also observed. These lesions were whitish-
gray and pitted in appearance, and were located
on the visceral rib surface near the rib head
adjacent to the pleura. The lesions, respectively
30 mm, 35 mm, and 25 mm in length, comprise
an area of approximately 30 cm mediolaterally
and 45 cm superiorly-inferiorly when considered
in anatomical position. The lesions are similar to

those described by Kelley and Micozzi (1984) as most likely being associated with primary pulmonary tuberculosis.

Differential diagnoses for rib lesions include typhoid, pyogenic osteomyelitis, syphilis, pleuritis, and other types of non-specific chronic respiratory disease (Kelley and Micozzi, 1984). If the rib and foot lesions are taken as one entity, an additional differential diagnosis is blastomycosis, although this fungus is not normally found in Connecticut (Mann and Murphy, 1990). Periostitic reaction resulting from the fracture of the left second rib can be ruled out because the healed fracture shows no osseous activity around the fracture site, which is located 11 cm from the lesion.

Regardless of the specific infectious etiology of pulmonary disease in this individual, symptoms of a chronic pulmonary infection severe enough to induce rib lesions would have probably included coughing, expectoration of mucous, and aches and pains of the chest. Such symptoms, if not actually caused by pulmonary tuberculosis, would likely have been interpreted as consumption by 19th century rural New Englanders.

No other cases of tuberculosis were noted in the remains from the cemetery. Two burials are believed to be related to "JB." Both burials, a 45- to 55-year-old female and a 13- to 14-year-old subadult, were buried in a manner similar to

"JB" and had the initials "IB-45" and "NB-13" spelled, respectively, in tacks on the coffin lid.

The Vampire Belief
To date, 12 historic accounts documenting vampire beliefs and activities in 18th and 19th century New England have been located. These accounts are found in southern and western Rhode Island, central-southern Vermont, southeastern Massachusetts, and eastern Connecticut, and range in time from the late 1700s to the late 1800s. Eleven of the 12 accounts denote consumption as the cause of death of the vampire and any deceased relatives.

The New England vampire belief is based on a folk interpretation of the physical appearance of the tuberculosis victim and the transmission of tuberculosis. As the name consumption implies, the disease caused sufferers to "waste away" and "lose flesh," despite the fact that they remained active, desirous of sustenance, and maintained a fierce will to live (Brown, 1941). This dichotomy of desire and "wasting away" is reflected in the vampire folk belief: The vampire's desire for "food" forces it to feed off living relatives, who suffer a similar "wasting away."

The vampire folklore tradition is also consistent with modern knowledge of the transmission of tuberculosis. Many of the historic accounts indicate that family members living in close association became infected with the disease before or soon after the death of the "vampire." Tuberculosis is notorious for being transmitted between individuals of different generations living under crowded conditions, a situation common in rural 19th century New England farming communities (Hawke, 1988). Seasonal periods of low nutrition and the unsanitary conditions of 18th and 19th century farming compounds increased the opportunity for transmission of tuberculosis between family members (Clark et al., 1987; Kelley and Eisenberg, 1987). Although there is no evidence of tuberculosis in the remaining Walton cemetery skeletons, an 1801 narrative of Griswold history indicates that during the 25 years preceding the account "consumptions have proved to be mortal to a number" (Phillips, 1929).

Killing the Vampire
The method of dispatching a vampire, also known as an apotropaic remedy, centers around the destruction of the vampire's body. In the New England folklore, if blood is found in the heart of the exhumed vampire, the apotropaic remedy was to burn the heart, in the process ridding the family of the vampire's actions. Most historic accounts indicate that upon exhuming the vampire, the body was found undecomposed and that blood was present in the heart. Barber's (1988) examination of the vampire belief in Europe indicates that the appearance of a vampire in the grave (i.e., bloating, hair and fingernails growing after death, the evidence of "blood" in the heart and chest) is attributable to the process of postmortem decomposition.

In the present case, however, the action is focused on the skeletal remains. Taphonomically, the physical arrangement of the skeletal remains in the grave indicates that no soft tissue had been present at the time of rearrangement; no heart remained in the body. We hypothesize that, in the absence of a heart to be burned, the apotropaic remedy was the place the bones in a "skull and crossbones" arrangement. In support of this hypothesis, we note that decapitation was a common European method of dispatching a dead vampire, and that the Celts and Neolithic Egyptians were known to separate the head from the body, supposedly to prevent the dead from doing harm (Barber, 1988).

Historical Evidence
Another piece of evidence is an historic newspaper account described in *The Book of Vampires* by Wright D in 1973. According to him: "In the May 20, 1854 issue of the Norwich (Connecticut) *Courier*, there is an account of an incident that occurred at Jewett, a city in that vicinity. About eight years previously, Horace Ray of Griswold had died of consumption. Afterwards, two of his children—adult sons— died of the same disease, the last one dying about 1852. Not long before the date of the newspaper the same fatal disease had seized another son, whereupon it was determined to exhume the bodies of the two brothers and burn them, because the dead were supposed to feed upon the living; and so long as the dead body in the grave remained undecomposed, either wholly

or in part, the surviving members of the family must continue to furnish substance on which the dead body could feed. Acting under the influence of this strange superstition, the family and friends of the deceased proceeded to the burial ground on June 8, 1854, dug up the bodies of the deceased brothers, and burned them on the spot."

This account places the vampire belief in the Jewett City/Griswold area just after the time span of the Griswold cemetery. The excellent preservation of the vampire skeleton indicates that it was probably buried toward the latter time period for the cemetery (ca. 1800–1840), thus placing the burial of this individual close to the time of the above account. The town of Griswold was settled just after 1812, in part by emigrants from Western Rhode Island, who were, according to local tradition, uneducated and "vicious" (Phillips, 1929). Note in Table 1 that several vampire accounts are also located in Western Rhode Island. The Rhode Island belief was examined by Stetson (1898), who relates that the Rhode Islanders he interviewed did not consider their practice to be vampirism but rather believed it was a way to protect living relatives from potential vampiristic actions of a deceased consumptive.

Conclusions

We present the following explanation for the bioarcheological and paleopathological evidence found in the grave in the Walton Cemetery. An adult male (J. B.) died of either tuberculosis or a pulmonary infection interpreted as tuberculosis (consumption) by his family. Several years after the burial, one or more of his family members contracted tuberculosis. They attributed their disease to the fact that J. B. had returned from the dead to "feed" upon them. To stop the progress of their disease, the body of the consumptive J. B. was exhumed so that the heart could be burned. Upon opening the grave, the family saw that the heart had decomposed. With no heart to burn, the bones of the chest were disrupted and the skull femora placed in a "skull and crossbones" position. This interpretation is based on three pieces of evidence: 1) the postmortem rearrangement of skeletal elements; 2) paleopathological evidence of tuberculosis or a chronic pulmonary infection producing similar physical manifestations; and 3) an historical account of the vampire folk belief from the same time and place as the skeleton under examination.

Chapter 7

1874, Ruth Ellen Rose, RI

At 53 years of age, William G. Rose was a man of action and a civic leader. As the first president of the local grange, he had a reputation for tackling adversity with an iron will and, when necessary, an iron fist.

William had recently lost his eldest daughter, Ruth Ellen, to a harsh fever. Ruth was born to William's first wife, Mary Taylor, who had died eight years earlier. Ruth had lingered for a while, giving her family hope for her recovery, but then, like a candle flame in a breeze, she was gone.

A few months after Ruth's passing, Rosalind, William's seven-year-old daughter began to show signs of the dreaded fever. Concerned that the malady might be more than a simple illness, William began to fear the presence of an unseen darkness preying on his children.

Initially, Rose sought help from the minister at the local chapel. Reverend Amos Cabot was a sturdy, meticulous man. He was surprised to see William Rose walking into his church on a Thursday afternoon. He knew William as a regular parishioner with his family on Sunday mornings, but had never thought of him as a particularly pious man. Cabot was of course aware of Ruth's recent death, and so it was not unheard of that the man might seek comfort in the house of God. Nonetheless Rose's appearance unnerved the priest, making the mild September day feel suddenly chill.

Reverend Cabot brought William into his small office at the back of the church, where the priest listened as William spoke of his suspicions. When he had finished, Reverend Cabot stood and moved to the window. For several minutes, he gazed out at the maple trees in the churchyard just outside, their crimson-tinged leaves moving gently in the breeze. *An early autumn*, mused the priest to himself.

Reverend Cabot turned back to face his desk. "Will, the loss of your daughter was a tremendous blow. I understand that." The priest moved again to the window, hands clutched behind his back. "But *vampires*? Maybe this madness has taken hold in other towns, but I cannot sanction such heretical notions here."

William leaned forward and placed his hands on the desk. "My little Rosalind is dying, Amos! Perhaps it's madness and perhaps it isn't, but I *cannot* take that chance!"

Cabot spun on him, his voice sharp. "Do you have any idea what this could do to our community? We can't lead people to believe that some ungodly creature is killing our children! People *die*, William. It's painful, but it happens!"

"What then would you have me do?"

"...Pray."

William was quaking now, his tone gone dark and low. "I'll be *damned* if I'm going to sit about grumbling at the heavens while some abomination is killing my family. Good day, Reverend Cabot."

"William..."

"Good day!"

Picking his hat up off the desk, William stood and walked out of the church. In his wake, the reverend fancied he could see the clouds of fury and desperation. When he had gone, Amos Cabot noticed that the day was indeed becoming overcast and much colder.

William was uncertain of how to act upon his theory. He began trying to seek out others who might know of or have experienced the terrible haunting that now afflicted his family, but no one to whom he spoke would claim knowledge of the subject. It was understood that they felt speaking of the evil could bring it down upon their own households. After weeks of fruitless research, William had come to believe that there was no way to stop the seething evil that was moving upon his family.

William had wed Mary Griswold, his second wife, several months after his first wife's death. Mary was also widowed, her former husband having been named Thomas Tillinghast.

One evening as William sat feeling weary and defeated, Mary came to his study.

"I need to speak to you, Will."

William looked up to see his handsome wife framed in the doorway, her usually strong face looking pale and haggard. She held her hands clutched in front of her, and there were dark circles around her eyes. When Mary spoke, her voice sounded distant, as though she were speaking through a heavy fog.

"My first husband died some time before I met you, William."

William was silent, waiting for her to continue. Mary's voice was tight and strained as she went on. "Thomas's family was not— *unfamiliar* — with the plague that is now afflicting us."

William looked as though he had been slapped. He pushed his chair back from the desk and stood. "I don't understand." William looked intently at his wife. "What are you saying?"

Mary came forward into the room and stood before the desk. She seemed about to speak again, then stopped.

"Mary please, I need to know what you mean!" William came around the desk and put his hands on his wife's arms. "Why will you not tell me?"

Mary collapsed into his arms and began to sob. She pressed herself against him like a fearful child clinging to its parent. "Oh god, William, when Ruth died I wanted to believe it was just a fever. But then little Rose got sick and you started talking of ghosts and devils, and..."

William gently held her away and looked into her face, his voice now calm and quiet. "Tell me about Thomas Tillinghast's family."

When Mary's story was done, William was heartsick with the fear that her words might be true. How could he accept such a terrible notion? She claimed that the wicked spirit could be laid to rest in only one way. The vampire was supposed to sleep in the grave of its last victim, in the very shape of the innocent whom it had destroyed. William's resolve nearly crumbled with the chilling revelation, but he needed only think of Rosalind's frail figure lying upstairs to find renewed courage. Convinced that defiling the resting place of his daughter was the only way to protect his family and the surrounding community from more suffering and death, he made a vow to go forward with the grisly task.

The afternoon sun stained the world scarlet as William walked up the gravel-covered lane toward the small family cemetery. He came to the wrought-iron gate, fashioned so long ago by his own grandfather, and looked beyond it at the spot where Ruth, the child he remembered as so full of life's boundless energy, lay cold beneath the soil. William sat on the granite step at the foot of the graveyard wall and wept.

Lost in his grief, William was startled from his reverie by a touch like that of a gentle hand on his shoulder. He looked up to see that the sky had grown black as pitch while he sat motionless upon the cold stone threshold of the burial ground. Before him stood a pale form, tall and slender, cloaked in hazy whiteness as though the very mists from the earth were spun into cloth.

"Father..." The misty figure breathed the words as if from a great distance.

William reached out a hand towards the shape. His voice quavered as he spoke. "Ruth?"

The figure extended one insubstantial hand toward William, touching his outstretched fingertips. The sensation was cold, and William became fearful that this apparition was not the daughter he had loved. Again came the distant plea, *"Father... I'm so cold...hold me father, ...I can't seem to get warm..."* The specter reached for him…

William sat up with a gasp to find himself alone at the cemetery gate. "A dream, only a dream…" he told himself as he shuddered with the damp chill of twilight, but he found himself doubting his own reassurances. The last crimson rays of the setting sun were still draining from the sky, taking with them the feeble warmth of the late autumn day.

Wiping the lingering dampness from his cheeks, William ascended the short stairs and entered the graveyard, each step crackling with a flurry of displaced leaves. Upon the ground before his daughter's headstone, he set his lamp, illuminating the markers around him and casting long shadows across the plot. Bending to his work, William bit his shovel into the earth over Ruth's grave and began to dig. The musty soil was still rather soft, having settled fairly little in the months since Ruth's burial. After a while, William's spade struck wood.

The casket was of good quality and showed little sign of decay. Apart from the scratches made by William while scraping it free of the earth, the lacquered lid was almost polished looking. Filthy and cold, William savagely broke the cover away with the edge of his shovel. Within the box lay a silent figure, anonymous in its white shroud. The only remarkable feature was the blood.

Spread across the cloth of the shroud was a great damp stain of blood. William recoiled in horror at the sight, and at the stench of death that issued forth from the ruptured box. Setting his jaw, he forced himself to picture his daughter Rosalind, as she lay sick and frail in her bed. "I cannot bear the loss of another child," he told himself. "Ruth would forgive me for this terrible thing I must do."

Pulling a large knife from the satchel he had brought, William placed it over the heart of his daughter, dimly thankful for the fetid shroud, which now concealed her face. Uttering an anguished cry, Ruth's father drove the blade into her unmoving form. From beneath the shroud came a terrible gasp — and then silence, apart from the whispering wind.

When William arrived home some time later, his wife was sitting in a rocking chair by the kitchen fire. Cradled in her arms was little Rosalind, asleep and peaceful. "Mary?"

Mrs. Rose looked up at her husband with weary eyes. "She's sleeping less fitfully Will, but the fever has not broken."

William moved to stand by the fire. His body was chilled throughout, and the warmth of the fire was almost painful. William looked at his wife as she sat quietly rocking their little girl. He spoke softly. "Now we wait."

Miraculously, Rosalind did indeed recover. She would never be a hearty child, but the mysterious fever relinquished its hold on her and never again troubled the Rose family of Peacedale.

Should you visit the Rose family cemetery on some quiet autumn day, you'll find the graves of William and Mary Rose shaded by an enormous beech tree. The tranquil spot gives little testimony to the strange goings-on that took place there over a century ago. There is no longer any evidence of the grave belonging to Ruth Ellen Rose. No stone marks the place where legend tells us that these tragic events occurred. Perhaps Mr. Rose couldn't bear to be reminded of the tragedy and had the marker removed. Perhaps the local minister would not allow Ruth to be returned to hallowed ground. Whatever the truth is, William and Ruth Ellen alone hold the secrets, and they aren't telling.

Records pertaining to the exhumation of the daughter of William Rose are scarce. The true identity of the suspected vampire is still a matter of debate. My initial investigations led me to a young woman named Juliet Rose, as related in my previous works on vampires. My choice to recast the vampire as Ruth Ellen is based on the exhaustive research and conclusions of Folklorist Michael Bell, New England's foremost authority on the topic.

Chapter 8

1892, Mercy Brown, RI "The Last Vampire"

March 18, 1892

Pale winter dawn is just staining the eastern horizon as a small group of men, silent in their dark coats and gloves, enter the hilltop graveyard. The trees surrounding the burial ground are little more than black silhouettes against the pink and grey light of the coming day. Frosty grass crackles beneath the boots of the somber procession as they approach their destination. Within a few moments, they stand before the squat stone crypt, and an older man at the front of the group places his lantern on the ground. A large iron key is produced from the breast pocket of his coat, and with a metallic groan—unnaturally loud in the pre-dawn stillness—the door of the tomb is thrust open.

The coffin rests upon a cart within the crypt. Frigid winter conditions have made burial in the family plot impossible until the coming of spring, when the ground will once again open to admit the dead. The lantern is carried into the small crypt and hung upon a bracket high on the back wall. Flickering shadows seem to come alive in the small chamber, dancing madly on the walls and ceiling.

Moving to the front of the group and entering the crypt behind the caretaker comes a young bespectacled man carrying a small black leather bag. In the yellow glow of the lantern's flame, his normally unremarkable face appears gaunt and sinister. His breath hangs misty in the chill of the early March air. A doctor by trade, he is here against his better judgment, praying that reason will prevail where only madness now holds court.

The others enter the tomb now, emboldened in the presence of this man of science. The doctor instructs the old caretaker to open the coffin. As each nail comes free from the ornate lid of the casket, a pained little screech echoes through the cramped chamber. The doctor removes a long thin scalpel from his bag, and gazing at the still form within the coffin, begins his work.

The crypt where Mercy Brown was interred 1892

Nine years earlier
The year 1883 was a harbinger of dark times for George Brown and his clan. Father to six children, Mr. Brown was a farmer who, like any country-born man of his kind, worked

hard and expected little more from life but to yield good crops, raise strong children, and keep peace with his neighbors. To see his daughters married off well and his son holding a good job was the height of his ambition, and until that autumn it seemed as though his hopes would come to pass.

Late in 1883, Mary, George's wife, began to show signs of illness. Mary was a strong woman—devoted to her family and used to hardship, being wife to a farmer. Despite her fortitude, consumption ravaged Mary's body, and on December 8th, 1883, she succumbed to the disease, closing her eyes forever. Faced with the difficult prospect maintaining his large family alone, George Brown had little time to grieve and so set about the task of putting his family's lives back in order.

By spring of the following year, Mary Olive, George's eldest daughter, had begun to fade. Complaining of fearful dreams and a crushing weight that drew the life out of her as she slept, she grew paler and more gaunt each night, until on June 6th, 1884, Olive joined her mother in eternal rest, leaving her father and siblings to wonder at the blight that afflicted their household.

Several years of relative peace followed for the people of the Brown farm. Edwin A., the only son of George and the late Mary Brown, was married and acquired a farm in nearby Wickford, where he hoped to make a life for himself and his bride. For a time, the shadow seemed to have passed the little Exeter family, but it was not to be.

A little more than five years after the death of Mary Olive, Edwin manifested the dreadful condition that had stolen his mother and sister from him. Terrible dreams of suffocation and drowning stole his rest, and in the mornings he felt as though the very blood had been drained from his body. Local doctors had no remedy for this mysterious plague, which was turning Edwin from a hearty young man into a pale, shaking scarecrow.

Friends advised the sickly Edwin to travel to Colorado Springs, hoping the well-known spa would help him to regain his health and vitality. Taking the proffered advice and pursued by bitter memories of his mother and sister, he and his wife headed west, praying for deliverance from the specter of death that haunted his family.

Edwin's convalescence in the west seemed to arrest the progress of the consumption for a time, but in January of 1892, misfortune struck once more. After almost two years of struggle with the disease, Edwin learned that Mercy Lena, his youngest sister, was taken with the malady. As though in response, his own condition began to worsen rapidly.

Edwin returned to Rhode Island upon learning of his sister's passing. The macabre events that followed were related to a shocked populace in the pages of the *Providence Journal*, March 19, 1892:

EXHUMED THE BODIES
Testing a horrible superstition in
the Town of Exeter.
BODIES OF DEAD RELATIVES TAKEN FROM
THEIR GRAVES

They had all died of consumption, and the belief was that live flesh and blood would be found that fed upon the bodies of the living.

Within a few years George T. Brown of Exeter has been bereft of a wife and two daughters by that dreaded disease consumption. His wife, Mary E., daughter of Pardon H. Arnold, was first stricken down about eight years ago, leaving her husband with six children, one son and five daughters. Within two years of the mother's death the eldest daughter, Olive B., died of the same disease, leaving the other members of the family apparently in good health. In a few years the son, Edwin A., who has been employed as a clerk by G. T. Cranston and by Taylor and Davis of Lafayette, was taken ill, and by advice of friends went to Colorado Springs about 18 months ago. During his absence the past winter another daughter, Mercy Lena, who appeared in good health at his departure, passed away after a few months of suffering. Three weeks ago Edwin A., finding his health so rapidly failing, came back to Rhode Island and now is critically ill at the residence of Willes Himes, his father-in-law.

During the few weeks past Mr. Brown has been besieged on all sides by a number of people, who expressed implicit faith in the old theory that by some unexplained and unreasonable way in some part of the deceased relative's body live flesh and blood might be found, which is supposed to feed on the living who are in feeble health. Mr. Brown, having no confidence in the old-time theory, and also getting no encouragement from the medical fraternity, did not yield to their importunities until Thursday afternoon, when an investigation was held under the direction of Harold Metcalf, M.D., of Wickford. The bodies of the wife and two daughters, who were buried in the Exeter Cemetery, were exhumed and an examination made, finding nothing but skeletons of the bodies of the wife and eldest daughter. After examination of the body of M. Lena, who was buried nine weeks ago, Dr. Metcalf reports the body in a state of natural decomposition, with nothing exceptional existing. When the doctor removed the heart and the liver from the body a quantity of blood dripped therefrom, but this he said was just what might be expected from a similar examination of almost any person after the same length of time from decease. The heart and liver were cremated by the attendants. Mr. Brown has the sympathy of the community.

[*Providence Journal*, 3/21/1892]

THE VAMPIRE THEORY

That search for the Spectral Ghoul
in the Exeter graves.
NOT A RHODE ISLAND TRADITION,
BUT SETTLED HERE

It originated in Europe: cremation of the heart of the sister for the consumptive brother to eat the ashes.

"Ugh!" says the person of refinement. "Horrible!" ejaculates even the reader of the horrible daily papers. But those who believe in it express themselves thus: "It may be true," "You may find one there," "I always heard it was so," and "My father and grandfather always said so." From traditions of the vampire, it is, on the whole, pleasant to be free, but how singular that this old belief of the Hindoos (sic) and Danubian peoples should survive in Rhode Island!

Had such a superstition been acted upon in White Russia or lower Hungary, Rhode Islanders would have read it as fiction, or a strange, wild falsehood. But this exhumation in the South County, in the town of Exeter, with the names of the persons authorizing it known in the county, and with a modern physician assisting, is a fact divested of mystery or fictional description. People who believed in the theory went to the medical examiner of the district, and he had the bodies exhumed, and examined them. It is probable that the theory was never practiced in this state under a better light of publicity, discussion and criticism.

Dr. Harold Metcalf, the medical examiner of the district, who examined the bodies, is a young and intelligent graduate of Bellevue. He is a Providence boy, and, after his graduation, located in this city (Providence), but three or four years ago removed to Wickford. He is not one to believe in the vampire superstition. He spent too long a time on the hospital-aid wagons which are sent into the

New York streets from Bellevue, to believe in anything relating to the human body which cannot be proven by the ordinary methods of medical science. He was called into the affair because he was the best physician nearest to Exeter, and examined the bodies because he was paid to do it. He in fact discouraged the suggestion, and affirmed that the result would be futile. He made his examination, as yesterday's *Journal* stated, without exceptional results, according to his own belief, but found in one of the bodies, to the satisfaction of many of the people down there, a sign which they regarded as the proof of their theory. When he removed the heart and liver from the body, a quantity of blood dripped therefrom. "The vampire," the attendants of the doctor said— and then, conforming to the theory of the necessity of destroying the vampire, burned the heart and liver. The people who urged the husband and father to exhume the bodies believe the vampire was found, and if the young man for whose sake the experiment was made recovers from his illness, they will, it is presumed, by reason of their acceptance of the truth of the tradition, consider the recovery due to the destruction of the spectral agent of his apparently fatal illness.

The vampire is described in the *Century Dictionary* as follows: "A kind of spectral being or ghost still possessing a human body, which, according to a superstition existing among the Slavic and other races of the lower Danube, leaves the grave during the night, and maintains a semblance of life by sucking the warm blood of men and women while they are asleep. Dead wizards, werewolves, heretics and other outcasts became vampires, and anyone killed by a vampire. On the discovery of a vampire's grave, the body, which it is supposed will be found fresh and ruddy, must be disinterred, thrust through with a whitethorn stake, and burned in order to render it harmless." In the *Encyclopedia Britannica* and other books a similar description of the vampire occurs. They all recount that the tradition comes from Europe, and did not originate with the Indians. Its earliest existence is said to have been in southwestern Russia, Servia, (sic) Poland and Bohemia. It is claimed also that it has prevailed to a certain extent in India, though the authorities at hand do not refer to this. The sole authority for the origin and prevalence of the idea outside of the Slavic peoples rests in stories written by two or three noted Frenchmen, and a number of less prominent English writers. From 1730–1735 the tradition took on renewed life, and starting in Hungary, spread all over Europe, and to America. At this time two of the principle books written upon the subject were published: Ranft's *De Masticatione Mortuorum in Tumulis Liber* and Calmet's *Dissertation on the Vampires of Hungary,* translated into English in 1750. The belief in the tradition was now marked by varying impressions on the form that the vampire took, and quite as variant opinions of the means necessary for the crushing of the power of the being or essence.

In all forms of the tradition, the vampire left its abode and wrought its object at night. When the full moon shone and the sky was cloudless, its opportunity was supposed to be most favorable. It left the body of the dead at the back of the neck, and appeared as a frog, toad, spider, bat or venomous fly from that moment until it returned to its corpse home. Its active moments when wandering about were spent in sucking the blood of the living, and this was invariably the blood of some relation or friend of the dead. From this feeding the body of the dead became fresh and rosy. Another form of the tradition, but with far less acceptance, was that the soul of the living man or woman left the body in his sleep in the shape of a straw or a fluff of down. It was wafted to the victim on the night breezes, and returned to the living without a warning of its visit, the victim being left pale and wan, and the vampire man being freshened and invigorated. Gautier has diverted the sense of the tradition to the plot of a powerful short story. For the eradication of the curse, the old method was always the digging up of the body of the dead, and the driving of a stake through the heart, the cutting off of the head, the tearing out and burning of the heart, or the pouring of boiling water and vinegar into the grave.

How the tradition got to Rhode Island and planted itself firmly here cannot be said. It was in existence in Connecticut and Maine 50 and 100 years ago, and the people of the South County say they got it from their ancestors, as far back in some cases as the beginning of the eighteenth century. The idea seems never to have been accepted in the northern part of the state, but every five or ten years it has cropped out in Coventry, West Greenwich, Exeter, Hopkinton, Richmond and the neighboring towns. In the case that has called out this reference to the subject, the principal persons interested were a farmer, George T. Brown, and his son Edwin A. Brown, a young man living near Shrub Hill, about two miles east of Pine Hill, which is the center of Exeter. The family had within four years suffered the loss of the wife and mother, four years ago; a daughter, Olive B., three years later; and Mercy Lena, another daughter, during the past winter. The son, Edwin A. Brown, was taken with the same disease, a harsh type of consumption, two years ago. His sister Lena became ill while he was in Colorado, where he had gone to improve his condition. Three weeks since, Edwin, finding his health fading, even in that favorite resort for consumptives, returned to Exeter. The local correspondent of the *Journal* tells the story of the call for Dr. Metcalf to hunt out the vampire, and of what occurred when the graves were searched, as follows:

"It seems that Dr. Metcalf attended Mercy Lena Brown during her last illness, and that a short time prior to her death he informed her father that further medical aid was useless, as the daughter, a girl of 18 or 19, was in the last stages of consumption. The doctor had heard nothing further from the family until a week ago when a man called on him and stated that Edwin A. Brown, the son, was in a dying condition from the same disease, and that several friends and neighbors fully believed that the only way in which his life could be saved was to have the bodies

92

of the mother and the two daughters exhumed, in order to ascertain if the heart in any of the bodies still contained blood, as these friends were fully convinced that if such were the case the dead body was living on the living tissue and blood of Edwin. The doctor sent the young man back, telling him the belief was absurd. Last Wednesday the man returned and told the doctor that Mr. Brown, the father, though not believing in the superstition himself, desired to have him come up to satisfy the neighbors, and make an autopsy of the bodies.

"On Wednesday morning therefore, the doctor went as desired to what is known as Shrub Hill Cemetery, in Exeter, and found four men, who had unearthed the remains of Mrs. Brown, who had been interred four years. Some of the muscles and flesh still existed in a mummified state, but there were no signs of blood in the heart. The body of the first daughter, Olive, was then taken out of the grave, but only a skeleton, with a thick growth of hair remained.

"Finally the body of Lena, the second daughter was removed from the tomb, where it had been placed till spring. The body was in a fairly well-preserved state. It had been buried two months. The heart and liver were removed and in cutting open the heart, clotted and decomposed blood was found, which was what might be expected at that stage of decomposition. The liver showed no blood, though it was in a well-preserved state. These two organs were removed, and a fire being kindled in the cemetery, they were reduced to ashes and the attendants seemed satisfied. The lungs showed diffuse tuberculosis germs. The old superstition of the natives of Exeter, and also believed in other farming communities, is either a vestige of the Black Art, or, as the people living here say, is a tradition of the Indians. And the belief is that, so long as the heart contains blood, so long will any of the immediate family who are suffering from consumption, continue to grow worse; but, if the heart is burned, that the patient will get better. And to make cure certain, the ashes of the heart and liver should be eaten by the person afflicted. In this case the doctor does not know if this latter remedy was resorted to or not, and he only knows from hearsay how ill the son Edwin is, never having been called to attend him."

All mention of "the vampire" is omitted from this account of the exhuming, but this signifies nothing. The correspondent simply failed to get to the bottom of the superstition. The files of the *Journal*, where reference is made in them to the practice of the tradition in Rhode Island, without exception speak of the search of the graves in such cases as attempts to discover the vampire. The last illustration of the practice was six or seven years ago in the same county, and it was then so described. Previous accounts of the digging up of bodies for the same purpose are also inspired by the vampire theory. Otherwise the analogy between this case and those which occurred in Europe in the 18th century is perfect, except in the confinement of the theory to a specific disease, and the terrible suggestion that the patient must take the ashes of the vampire internally to be cured. These ideas are not, so far as can be learned, based on any form of the European tradition. The books and authorities of Europe do not connect the theory with consumption, nor, in its legend, turn upon that application, with the victim's eating the vampire. This presentation of the theory must be of American or Rhode Island origin, and most likely it can be claimed as the exclusive possession of Rhode Island's country people. It is horrible to contemplate, and the local correspondent can hardly be blamed for attributing it to the Indians. It seems very odd that the South County people alone should ever have re-gendered and accepted such fancies.

A little may be added to the story upon the medical side. The family was not hereditarily consumptive, but consumption is, of course, liable to start from causes besides family predisposition. The physicians, on the other hand, are unwilling to affirm that it is invariably contagious, but assert that it abounds from causes closely allied to the operation of a contagion. For example, a person remaining in the room with a consumptive, attending upon such a sufferer in his or her illness, or living subsequent to the death of a consumptive under the same hygienic conditions, is generally considered to be in danger of the disease. Thus in the case of this family, even providing the children did not take the disease from a hereditary susceptibility to it, they were subjected to its influences, for they all lived in the farm house with their mother when she died. The daughter nursed her, and by the time the son took it, he had been under its fatal power according to intensified, if not multiplied, circumstances of danger. In regard to the blood and the condition of the heart of the daughter Lena, who had been dead but two months, Dr. Metcalf's statement that the blood and the unexhausted molecular composition of the heart were not signs of a state of affairs at all unusual, will be borne out by any good physician, for it is well known that the heart, the fountain of the blood, usually retains till the final time of decomposition the semblances of its function.

Dr. Metcalf made his autopsies in the cemetery before the men who had been employed in digging up the bodies, and they, according to the doctor's story, as told by the correspondent, appeared satisfied that the cause of Edwin Brown's illness, or the remedy for his cure, had been found. They had believed that a vampire lay in one of the bodies; they had searched for it; they had found it. If the sick man is now cured by the adoption of these means, which includes his absorption of the cremated heart of his sister, it is assumed that, believing as these people do, they will assign the cause of returning health to the remedy they adopted. What therefore is one to say? It is a temptation to treat the whole affair as something ridiculous, but if it be so regarded, the facts in the case likewise suggest the most sorrowful and hideous of pictures. To write and interpret the facts in their unvarnished form, here in this city, but 25 miles from the scene, is a task requiring imaginativeness almost sufficient to cover an inhuman rite of the Africans of the upper Congo, or to compass one of Rider Haggard's most thrilling chapters.

The grave of Mercy Lena Brown

A letter appearing in the Pawtuxet Valley Gleaner a few weeks after Mercy's exhumation supplies an epilogue to the above account concerning Edwin Brown's fate. Sadly, it confirms the ineffectiveness of the prescribed remedy.

Mr. Editor,
As considerable notoriety has resulted from the exhuming of three bodies in Exeter Cemetery on 17th inst., I will give the main facts as I have received them for the benefit of such of your readers as "have not taken the papers" containing the same.

To begin, we will say that our neighbor, a good and respectable citizen, George T. Brown, has been bereft of his wife and two grown-up daughters by consumption— the wife about 8 years ago, and the eldest daughter, Olive, two years or so later. The other daughter, Mercy Lena, died about two months since, after nearly one year's illness from the same dread disease. About two years ago Mr. Brown's only son Edwin A., a young married man of good habits, began to give evidence of lung trouble which increased, until in hopes of checking and curing the same, he was induced to visit the famous Colorado Springs where his wife followed him later on. While over a time he seemed to improve, it soon became evident that there was no real benefit derived, and this coupled with a strong desire on the part of both husband and wife to see their Rhode Island friends, they decided to return East after an absence of about 18 months. They are staying with Mrs. Brown's parents, Mr. and Mrs. Willett Himes.

We are sorry to say that Eddie's health is not encouraging at this time. And now comes the queer part, it is: the revival of superstitions regarding the feeding of the dead upon a living relative, where consumption was the cause of death, and so bringing the living person soon into a similar condition. To avoid this result, according to the same high authority, the "vampire" in question which is said to inhabit the heart of a dead consumptive while any blood remains in that organ, must be cremated and the ashes carefully preserved and administered in some form to the living victim, when a speedy cure may (un)reasonably be expected. I will here say that the husband and father of the deceased ones has, from the first, disclaimed any faith at all in the vampire theory, but being urged, he allowed other, if not wiser, counsel to prevail. On the 17th inst., as before stated, the three bodies alluded to were exhumed and then examined by Dr. Metcalf of Wickford (under protest, as it were, being an unbeliever).

The two bodies longest buried were found decayed and bloodless, while the last one who has been only about two months buried showed some blood in the heart as a matter of course, and as the Doctor expected. To carry out what was a foregone conclusion the heart and lungs of the last named (M. Lena) were then and there duly cremated, but deponent saith not how the ashes were disposed of. Not many persons were present, Mr. Brown being among the absent ones. While we do not blame anyone for their proceedings, as they were intended without doubt to relieve the anxiety of living, still it seems incredible, that anyone can attach the least importance to the subject, being so entirely incompatible with reason.

The graves of the Brown Family

Unarguably the best known incident of historical vampirism in America, the story of Mercy Brown has resonated through the folklore and imagination of people throughout the world. Mercy's grave attracts hundreds of visitors from around the country each year, and her story has inspired some of the most notable authors of horror fiction, from H. P. Lovecraft's *The Shunned House* to Bram Stoker's immortal classic *Dracula*.

Chapter 9

Whispers from the Dead

The towns and valleys of New England are peppered with elusive fragments and vague accounts of the vampire legend. Some of these leads are so obscure as to seem untraceable, while others endlessly recycle the same handful of misleading information. Occasionally, however, a fragment provides the beginnings of a worthy tale.

Plymouth, MA, 1807
Old Colony Memorial and Plymouth County Advertiser, 1822

In that almost insulated part of the state of Massachusetts, called *Old Colony* or *Plymouth Colony*, and particularly in a small village adjoining the shire town, there may be found the relics of many old customs and superstitions which would be amusing, at least to the antiquary. Among others of less serious cast, there was, 15 years ago, one which, on account of its peculiarities, and its consequence, I beg leave to mention. It is well known to those who are acquainted with that section of our country, that nearly one-half of its inhabitants die of consumption, occasioned by the chilly humidity of their atmosphere, and the long prevalence of easterly winds. The inhabitants of this village (or town as it is there called) to which I allude were peculiarly exposed to this scourge; and I have seen, at one time, one of every 50 of its inhabitants gliding down to the grave with all the certainty which characterizes this insidious foe of the human family.

There was, 15 years ago, and is perhaps at this time, an opinion prevalent among the inhabitants of this town, that the body of a person who died of consumption was, by some supernatural means, nourished in the grave by some living member of the family; and that during the life of this person, the body retained, in the grave, all the fullness and freshness of life and health. This belief was strengthened by the circumstance that whole families frequently fell prey to this terrible disease.

Of one large family in this town, consisting of 14 children, and their venerable parents, the mother and the youngest son only remained— the rest within a year of each other had died of consumption. Within two months from the death of the 13th child, an amiable girl of about 16 years of age, the bloom, which characterized the whole of this family, was seen to fade from the cheek of the last support of the heart-smitten mother, and his broad flat chest was occasionally convulsed by the powerful deep coughing which attends consumption in our Atlantic states.

At this time, as if to snatch one of the family from an early grave, it was resolved by a few of the inhabitants of the village to test the truth of this tradition which I have mentioned, and which the circumstances of this afflicted family seemed to confirm. I should have added that it was believed that if the body thus supernaturally nourished in the grave should be raised and turned over in the coffin, its depredation upon the survivor would necessarily cease. The consent of the mother being obtained, it was agreed that four persons, attended by the surviving and complaining brother, should, at sunrise the next day, dig up the remains of the last buried sister. At the appointed hour they attended in the burying yard, and having with much exertion removed the earth, they raised the coffin upon the ground; then, displacing the flat lid, they lifted the covering from her face, and discovered what they had indeed anticipated, but dreaded to declare. "Yes, I saw the visage of one who had been long the tenant of a silent grave, lit up with the brilliancy of youthful health. The cheek was full to dimpling, and a rich profusion of hair shaded her cold forehead, while some of its richest curls floated upon her unconscious breast. The large blue eyes had scarcely lost their brilliancy, and the livid fullness of her red lips seemed almost to say, *'loose me and let me go.*"

In two weeks, the brother, shocked with the spectacle he had witnessed, sunk under his disease. The mother survived scarcely a year, and the long range of 16 graves is pointed out to the stranger as evidence of the truth of the belief of the inhabitants. The following lines were written on a recollection of the above shocking scene:

I saw her, the grave sheet was 'round her,
Months had passed since they laid her in the clay;
Yet the damps of the tomb could not wound her,
The worms had not seized on their prey.
Oh, fair was her cheek, as I knew it.
When the rose all its colors there brought;
And that eye,—did a tear then bedew it?
It gleam'd like the herald of thought.
She bloom'd, though the shroud was around her,
Her locks o'er her her cold bosom wave,
As if the stern monarch had crown'd her,
The fair speechless queen of the grave.
But what lends the grave such a luster?
O'er her cheeks what such beauty had shed?
His life's blood, who bent there, had nurs'd her,
The living was food for the dead!

Dummerston, VT, 1778

This curious fragment, from D. Mansfield's *History of the Town of Dummerston*, clearly falls within the realm of vampirism, though it may be the first time in history that the suspected progenitor of the curse was a plant!

Lieutenant Leonard Spaulding was born Oct. 28, 1728, and died of consumption July 17th, 1788. He was buried at his own request in the graveyard east of the hollow, because at that time, the cemetery where his children were buried was wet ground. No stone marks his resting-place. Although the children of Lieutenant Spaulding, especially the sons, became large muscular persons, all but one or two died under 40 years of age of consumption, and their sickness was brief.

It is related by those who remember the circumstance; after six or seven of the family had died of consumption, another daughter was taken, it was supposed, with the same disease. It was thought she would die, and much was said in regard to so many of the family dying of consumption when they all seemed to have the appearance of good health and long life. Among the superstitions of those days, we find it was said that a vine or root of some kind grew from coffin to coffin of those of one family who died of consumption, and were buried side-by-side; and when the growing vine had reached the coffin of the last one buried, another of the family would die. The only way to destroy the influence or effect was to break the vine, take up the body of the last one, and burn the vitals, which would be an effectual remedy. Accordingly, the body of the last one buried was dug up and the vitals were taken out and burnt, and the daughter, it is affirmed, got well and lived many years. The act doubtless raised her mind from the state of the despondency to hopefulness.

Griswold/Jewett City, CT, 1854

Modern 'vampires' seldom trouble society, so far as narratives tell; but in recent years something of the kind has occupied public attention within the limits of the present generation. The *Norwich Courier* of May 20th, 1854, tells of an event that occurred on May 8, 1854. The father and two sons of the Ray family of Griswold, CT, had died of "consumption." Lemuel Ray died first, in 1845; his father, Henry Baker Ray (referred to as 'Horace' in the *Courier* account), died in 1849, and Lemuel's brother Elisha followed in 1851. When a third brother, Henry Nelson Ray, was felled by the dread disease, the family, evidently having the vampyre theory in their thoughts, determined to exhume the bodies of the first two deceased. If the dead bodies remained in a fresh or semi-fresh state, all the vampire mischief would be produced, the supposition being that the dead had been feeding on the living. They journeyed to the cemetery in Jewett City with some friends, dug up the bodies of Lemuel and Elisha, and "burned them on the spot." Their work was in vain, however, for Henry Nelson Ray died on September 1st of the same year. Henry's daughter Nettie was also a victim of the "vampire," dying by the age of 26.

West Greenwich, RI, 1889

The persistence of the "Vampire's Grave" legend in rural Rhode Island demonstrates the ability of a story fragment to evolve into the status of a full-blown urban legend.

Often when I am speaking in my home state of Rhode Island on the subject Yankee vampire legends, some enthusiastic listener will ask, "What do you know about 'Vampire's Grave'?" It is always phrased that way, like a proper name, as though a sign existed at some cemetery entrance welcoming visitors to "Vampire's Grave," Rhode Island.

Despite the vagueness of these inquiries, I am always immediately certain what gravesite they are referring to. Situated a few miles down the twisting, rural Plain Meeting House Road is an old cemetery surrounded by a low stone wall. Adjacent to the church that gives the road its name, the graveyard is fairly large, with burials dating from the 1700s to the present.

A short tour of this historical site reveals a number of notable people, but also an inordinate number of overturned and broken stones. Some of this is no doubt accidental or environmental in nature, but much of the damage is caused by the droves of "vampire seekers" who flock to the site on a regular basis. The grave that they come in search of is that of Nellie L. Vaughn, who died in 1889 at the age of nineteen. In the last few decades, Nellie has become the center of a vampire legend that has nearly eclipsed the many other such regional stories.

Nellie's often-recounted tale reads much like the others. It features a young girl who dies of a wasting fever, nightly visitations by a ghostly figure, and the eventual exhumation and removal of the girl's heart. As Nellie's legend has grown over the years, people have reported a persistence of odd and uncanny phenomena. Modern accounts claim that no vegetation will grow on the vampire's grave. Odd lights and disembodied voices are said to emanate from the ground near Nellie's stone. In recent years, an attempt was even made by persons unknown to exhume a corpse from the cemetery.

All these events seem to spring from popular legends of Nellie's existence as a vampire. In this instance however, the legends are patently untrue. To put it bluntly, Nellie was "framed." While southern New England *is* rich with genuine vampire folklore, Nellie's reputation as one of the undead does not appear to extend farther back than 35 or 40 years. According to most accounts, sometime in the mid-1960s, a Coventry High School teacher related some of the region's vampire folklore to one of his classes. When pressed for the location of the "Vampire's Grave," he said only that it was off Victory Highway, also known as Rt.102.

A few of the students were undaunted by the vagueness of the teacher's reply. They had been told that the vampire was a woman and had been about 19 or 20 at the time of her death. Armed with flashlights and a sense of adventure, they set off in search of the vampire's resting place.

No one can say how long the students looked for the grave, but at some point someone stumbled upon the eerily secluded Plain Meeting House graveyard. There, among the dozens of similar graves, was the stone of Nellie L. Vaughn.

Nellie had indeed died at the age of nineteen, and on her stone was the haunting inscription,

"I am Watching and Waiting for you."

No further evidence was needed to convict Nellie. The search was over for the intrepid vampire hunters, and a new legend was born.

The Plain Meeting House Cemetery is visited constantly even today by curiosity seekers on the trail of the "Vampire's Grave."

It is impossible to know precisely which legend the Coventry teacher had been referring to. Most likely he had related the story of Exeter's Mercy Brown, the best known of Rhode Island's vampire tales. Even the teacher may have been uncertain of the name or location of the alleged vampire. Many of the area's vampire legends have been blurred into one another so that details and specifics are almost indistinguishable from story to story.

Nellie Vaughn's gravestone at the Plain Meeting House Cemetery is no longer standing, having been destroyed by vandalism. Irreparable damage has been done to both the burial ground and the adjacent church. Visitors to the site should please keep this in mind and visit only during daylight hours. Local police will eject anyone found at the site after dark.

Chapter 10

Dracula Meets the Yankees

Rolling hills are splashed with the gold and crimson of autumn. Small towns are abuzz with activity as preparations are made for winter. Farmers load their wagons with pumpkins and corn, and head for the harvest fairs and country markets that abound. Over each village, a church spire is visible, and a pleasant smoky scent fills the air. As I drive through this pleasant land, I am homesick for a similar life in my native New England. Here however, I am a stranger. I have come to this land in search of the most infamous vampire in history. It is October 31st, 1996—and I am in Transylvania.

I round a curve on this serpentine mountain road, and my heart skips a beat at the sight before me. Berta, my stalwart traveling photographer is speechless. I search for an eloquent phrase to express the moment... *"Wow."*

Castle Dracula looms before us, its dusty gray bulk perched atop a nearly barren mountain ridge. We have reached our destination. The late afternoon sun is precariously low— sunset comes early in the mountains. Tonight is Halloween, and Castle Dracula is having guests for dinner!

Transylvania is a vast hilly region cradled in the irregular horseshoe of Romania's Carpathian Mountains. The Transylvanians are some of the finest pastry makers in Europe, and the area's craftsmen are among the most skilled in the world. It is home to some of the most well-preserved medieval cities left in Europe today. It is also home to Dracula.

Photographer Berta Daniels and the author
at Castle Dracula Arefu, Romania, 1996

In spring of the year 1897, a lumbering bear of an Irishman named Bram (short for Abraham) Stoker published the novel that would define the word *vampire* to over a century of readers. Inspired by tales of the bloodthirsty Transylvanian prince, Stoker wove history and legend together into the story of the vampire king: *Dracula*.

Before we delve into Dracula's influence on American vampire lore, we should explore a bit of the novel's 100-year legacy. Since its publication at the close of the Victorian era, the novel *Dracula* has never been out of print—a rare distinction shared by only a few other books, including the Bible. Dracula's epic storyline concerns the notorious Count's attempt to abandon his native Transylvania in order to hunt unhindered among the teeming populace of an unwary London. In Stoker's original novel, the Count is eventually defeated by a motley band of Victorian-era vampire hunters. Count Dracula proved more resilient than Stoker imagined him, however, and was revived to play the villain (and occasionally the hero) in hundreds of novels, films, and plays in the century since his first demise.

In addition to his role as the eternally resurrecting "King of Vampires," Dracula has been largely responsible for the development of the modern image of vampirism. Recurring elements of the vampire myth such as fangs, bats, shape-changing, and black cloaks are a direct carry over from Dracula's many early incarnations. Later authors, from Stephen King to Anne Rice, have used the ground rules established by Stoker's *Dracula* as the basis for all of their vampire tales. Bram Stoker's own inspiration for Dracula was a melting pot of myth, history, and mid-19th-century gothic drama. The figure of Count Dracula himself is based largely on the 15th-century Transylvanian warlord-prince Vlad Dracula.

Vlad Dracula, known also as Vlad the Impaler, was born in 1431 in the Transylvanian town of Sighisoara. He was the son of Prince Vlad Dracul. Situated in the heart of the Carpathian

Mountains, Transylvania and its sister principalities Wallachia and Moldavia make up the area of modern day Romania. Dracul and his descendants earned their surname in 1431 when the elder Vlad was inducted as a knight of the Order of the Dragon ("Dracul" in Romanian). Young Dracula ("Son of the Dragon"), having been born that same year, was given the birthright of his father's knighthood.

The Transylvanian Prince Dracula

Dracula's life was fated to follow a violent path. As a young boy, his father's enemy, the Turkish Sultan Murad, made him a political prisoner. Following the elder Dracul's assassination, the 17-year-old Dracula was given his father's throne to act as a puppet prince for the Sultan. Soon after ascending to the throne, however, Dracula turned against the Sultan, thus formally beginning his personal vendetta against the Ottoman Empire, which would drive him for the remainder of his days.

Though considered in life to have been one of the most ruthless and formidable military tacticians of his time, the historical Dracula was never believed to be a vampire. Dracula was reportedly ambushed and assassinated in 1476 in the marshes near the monastery of Snagov. Dracula's tomb lies beneath a stone slab near Snagov's altar. Rumors persist that an archaeologist in the 1930s opened the tomb and found it empty, but the monks who guard Dracula's grave even today will tell you that the story is only a myth.

Four hundred and twenty years after Dracula's reported death, Bram Stoker was traveling in America as the manager of British actor Henry Irving. Stoker had published several works of fiction by 1896 but had not seen much success in his literary career. One project, which Stoker had been toying with for some time, was an ambitious vampire story set in modern day. Bram had already established the basic elements of his tale, and had chosen to model his undead villain on a little-known Romanian nobleman whose bloodthirsty deeds were legendary in his homeland. Unfortunately, Stoker was uncertain that another book was wise, given the lackluster response to his previous works. Putting himself on the line with a tawdry gothic thriller seemed like an unwise move under the circumstances.

Stoker's doubts about the salability of the vampire theme might have laid Count Dracula to a premature rest had he not stumbled across a choice bit of information while in America. During an 1896 engagement in Philadelphia, Stoker received a startling clipping from a current issue of a New York newspaper, *The World*:

VAMPIRES IN NEW ENGLAND

Dead bodies dug up and their hearts burned to prevent disease.

Strange superstition of long ago.

The old belief was that ghostly monsters sucked the blood of their living relatives.

Recent ethnological research has disclosed something very extraordinary in Rhode Island. It appears that the ancient vampire superstition still survives in that state, and within the last few years, many people have been digging up the dead bodies of relatives for the purposes of burning their hearts.

Near Newport, scores of such exhumations have been made, the purpose being to prevent the dead from preying upon the living. The belief entertained is that a person who has died of consumption is likely to rise from the grave at night and suck the blood of surviving members of his or her family, thus dooming them to a similar fate. The discovery of this survival in highly educated New England of a superstition dating back to the days of Sardanapalus and Nebuchadnezzar has been made by George R. Stetson, an ethnologist of repute. He has found it rampant in the district which includes the towns of Exeter, Foster, Kingstown, East Greenwich and many scattered hamlets. This region, where abandoned farms are numerous, is the stamping ground of the book agent, the chromo peddler, and the patent medicine man. The social isolation is as complete as it was two centuries ago.

Here Cotton Mather and the host of medical, clerical, and lay believers in the uncanny ideas of bygone centuries could still hold high carnival. Not merely the out-of-the-way agricultural folk, but the more intelligent people of the urban communities are strong in their belief in vampirism. One case noted was that of an intelligent and well-to-do head of a family who some years ago lost several of his children by consumption. After they were buried he dug them up and burned them in order to save the lives of their surviving brothers and sisters.

TWO TYPICAL CASES

There is one small village distant fifteen miles from Newport, where within the last few years there have been at least half a dozen resurrections on this account. The most recent was made two years ago in a family where the mother and four children had already succumbed to consumption. The last of these children was exhumed and the heart was burned.

Another instance was noted in a seashore town, not far from Newport, possessing a summer hotel and a few cottages of hot weather residents. An intelligent man, by trade a mason, informed Mr. Stetson that he had lost two brothers by consumption. On the death of the second brother his father was advised to take up the body and burn the heart. He refused to do so, and consequently was attacked by the disease. Finally he died of it. His heart was burned, and in this way the rest of the family escaped.

This frightful superstition is said to prevail in all of the isolated districts of southern Rhode Island, and it survives to some extent in the large centers of population. Sometimes the body is burned, not merely the heart, and the ashes are scattered.

In some parts of Europe this belief still has a hold on the popular mind. On the Continent from 1717 to 1735 there prevailed an epidemic of vampires. Thousands of people died, as was supposed, by having their blood sucked by creatures that came to their bedsides at night with goggling eyes and lips eager for the life fluid of the victim. In Servia it was understood that the demon might be destroyed by digging up the body and piercing it through with a sharp instrument, after which it was decapitated and burned. Relief was found in eating the earth of the vampire's grave. In the Levant the corpse was cut to pieces and boiled in wine.

VAMPIRISM A PLAGUE

There was no hope for a person once chosen as a prey by a vampire. Slowly but surely he or she was destined to fade and sicken, receiving meanwhile nightly visits from the monster. Even death was no relief, for— and here was the most horrible part of the superstition— the victim, once dead and in the grave, was compelled to become a vampire and in his turn to take up the business of preying on the living. Thus vampirism was indefinitely propagated.

Realise, if you please, that at that period when science was hardly born, and no knowledge had been spread among the people to fight off superstition, belief in the reality of this fearful thing was absolute. Its existence was officially recognised, and military commissions were appointed for the purpose of opening the graves of suspected vampires and taking such measures as were necessary for destroying the latter.

Vampirism became a plague, more dreaded than any form of disease. Everywhere people were dying from the attacks of the blood-sucking monsters, each victim in turn becoming a night-prowler in pursuit of human prey. Terror of the mysterious and unearthly peril filled all hearts.

Evidence enough as to the prevalence of the mischief was afforded by the condition of many of the bodies that were dug up by the commissions appointed for the purpose. In many instances corpses which had been buried for weeks and even months were found fresh and lifelike. Sometimes fresh blood was actually discovered on their lips. What proof could be more convincing, inasmuch, as was well known, the buried body of a vampire is preserved and nourished by its nightly repasts? The blood on the lips, of course, was that of the victim of the night before.

The faith in vampirism entertained by the public at large was as complete as that which is felt in a discovery of modern science. It was an actual epidemic that threatened the people, spreading rapidly and only to be checked by the adoption of the most drastic measures.

The contents of every suspected grave were investigated, and many corpses found in such a condition as that described were promptly subjected to "treatment." This meant that a stake was driven through the chest, and the heart, being taken out, was either burned or chopped into small pieces, for in this way only could a vampire be deprived of power to do mischief. In one case a man who was unburied sat up in his coffin, with fresh blood on his lips. The official in charge of the ceremonies held a crucifix before his face and saying, "Do you recognize your saviour?" chopped the unfortunate's head off. This person presumably had been buried alive in a cataleptic trance.

WERE THEY BURIED ALIVE?

How is the phenomenon to be accounted for? Nobody can say with certainty, but it may be that the fright tale that people were thrown by the epidemic had the effect of predisposing nervous people to catalepsy. In a word, people were buried alive in a condition where the vital function being suspended, they remained, as it were, dead for a while. It is a common thing for a cataleptic to bleed at the mouth just before returning to consciousness. According to the popular superstition, the vampire left his or her body in the grave, while engaged in nocturnal prowls.

The epidemic prevailed all over south-eastern Europe, being at its worst in Hungary and Servia. It is supposed to have originated in Greece, where a belief was entertained to the effect that Latin Christians buried in that country, could not decay in their graves, being under the ban of the Greek church. The cheerful notion was that they got out of their graves at night, and pursued the occupation of ghouls. The superstition as to ghouls is very ancient, and undoubtedly of Oriental origin. Generally speaking however, a ghoul is just the opposite of a vampire, being a living person who preys on dead bodies, while a vampire is a dead person that feeds on the blood of the living. If you had your choice, which would you rather be, a vampire, or a ghoul?

One of the most familiar of the stories of the Arabian nights tells of a woman who annoyed her husband very much by refusing food. Nothing more than a few grains of rice would she eat at meals. He discovered that she was in the habit of stealing away from his side in the night, and following her on one such occasion, he found her engaged in digging up and devouring a corpse.

Among the numerous folk tales about vampires is one relating to a fiend named Dakanavar, who dwelt in a cave in Armenia. He would not permit anybody to penetrate into the mountains of Ulmish (Illegible word) or to count their valleys. Everyone who attempted this had in the night the blood sucked from the soles of his feet until he died.

At last however he was outwitted by two cunning fellows. They began to count the valleys, and when night came they lay down to sleep, taking care to place themselves with the feet of each under the head of the other. In the night the monster came, felt as usual and found a head. Then he felt at the other end and found a head there also.

"Well," cried he, "I have gone through all of the three hundred and sixty-six valleys of these mountains, and have sucked the blood of people without end, but never yet did I find one with two heads and no feet!" So saying he ran away and was never more seen in that country, but ever since people have known that the mountains have three hundred and sixty-six valleys.

Belief in the Vampire Bats is more modern. For a long time it was ridiculed by science as a delusion, but it has been proved to be founded correctly upon fact. It was the famous naturalist Darwin who settled this question. One

118

night he was camping with a party near Coquimbo, in Chile, and it happened that a servant noticed the restlessness of one of the horses. The man went up to the horse and actually caught a bat in the act of sucking blood from the flank of the animal.

The 1896 Newspaper clipping that inspired Bram Stoker's work on the novel *Dracula*

While many kinds of bats have been ignorantly accused of the blood-sucking habit, only one species is really a vampire. It constitutes a genus all by itself. Just as a man is the only species of the genus Homo, so the vampire bat is the only species of the genus Desmodus. Fortunately it is not very large, with a wingspread of only two feet. This is not much for a bat. The so called "Flying Foxes" of the old world, which go about in flocks and ravage orchards, are of much greater size, and there is a bat of Java known as the "Kalong" that has a spread of five feet from wing-tip to wing-tip. The body of the true Vampire Bat weighs only a few ounces.

The preceding article was discovered among Stoker's research notes for *Dracula*. Clearly drawing heavily on Stetson's *Animistic Vampire in New England*, it contains references to a number of events that foreshadow elements of Stoker's unpublished novel. Dracula's transformation into a bat (not previously established as a convention of the genre) and the setting of Jonathan and Mina Harker's home in the namesake town of Exeter are worthy of note, but the death and vampiric resurrection of Lucy Westenra is perhaps the most striking, bearing a strong resemblance to the events in the Mercy Brown case of only a few years earlier. Consider these passages from the pages of *Dracula*, as he describes the transformation of Lucy into one of the undead:

> She was ghastly, chalkily pale; the red seemed to have gone even from her lips and gums, and the bones of her face stood out prominently; her breathing was painful to see or hear...

The attentions of a physician do no good, and Lucy dies. Soon thereafter, reports of a lovely lady stealing children away by night reach the ears of Lucy's loved ones, and though they protest, they are forced to accept that Lucy is behind the attacks. Entering her tomb, they make a grisly discovery:

Outrageous as it was to open a leaden coffin, to see if a woman dead nearly a week were really dead, it now seemed the height of folly to open the tomb again....Van Helsing walked over to Lucy's coffin, and I followed. He bent over and forced back the leaden flange; and then a shock of surprise and dismay shot through me... There lay Lucy, seemingly just as we had seen her the night before her funeral. She was, if possible, more radiantly beautiful than ever; and I could not believe she was dead...

Comparison can even be made between the names Mercy and Lucy, although it is not certain that Stoker's research into the New England vampire incidents put him on a first name basis with the "Vampire of Exeter." We do know that he went on to create the most enduring vampire character in literary history, and it seems quite likely that the contemporary legends of New England's own restless dead may be responsible for this resurrection!

Chapter 11

Romanian Folk Remedies in the New World

The appearance of the vampire legend on American shores remains a mystery to folklorists and historians alike. The vampire epidemics of Western Europe began long after the colonies were settled, and Eastern Europeans did not begin to emigrate to the New World until the middle of the 19th century, when New England's vampire scare was already well underway. Some have suggested that the legend (which was not known in America by the term "vampire" until well into the 1880s) was spontaneous in origin—a natural response to the ravages of an unknown disease. This theory is challenged by the information in the following excerpt. The parallels between the vampire remedies of the Romania, birthplace of the legendary Dracula, and that of early New Englanders argues strongly against the possibility of coincidence.

The Vampire in Roumania
By Agnes Murgoci, Ph.D.,
Presented May 4th, 1927

The folklore of vampires is of special interest from the light it throws on primitive ideas about body and soul, and about the relation of the body and soul after death.

In Russia, Roumania, and the Balkan States there is an idea— sometimes vague, sometimes fairly definite— that the soul does not finally leave the body and enter into Paradise until forty days after death. It is then supposed that it may even linger for years, and when this is the case decomposition is delayed. In Roumania, bodies are disinterred at an interval of three years after death in the case of a child, of four or five years in the case of young folk, and of seven years in the case of elderly people. If decomposition is not then complete, it is supposed that the corpse is a vampire; if it is complete, and the bones are white and clean, it is a sign that the soul has entered into eternal rest. The bones are washed in water and wine and put in clean linen, a religious service is held, and they are re-interred.

In Bukovina and the surrounding districts there was an orgy of burials and re-burials in the years 1919 and 1920, for not only were people dying of epidemics and hardships, but the people who had died in the early years of the War had to be disinterred.

It is now considered to be the exceptional that a spirit should reanimate its body and walk as a vampire, but in a vampire story quoted below, it is said that they were once as common as blades of grass. It would seem that the most primitive phase of the vampire belief was that all departed spirits wished evil to those left, and that special means had to be taken in all cases to prevent their return. The most typical vampire is therefore the reanimated corpse. We may call this the dead-vampire type.

People destined to become vampires after death may be able in life to send out their souls, and leave their bodies, to wander at crossroads with the reanimated corpses. This type may be called the live-vampire type. It merges into the ordinary witch or wizard, who can meet other witches or wizards either in the body or as a spirit. A third type of vampire is the varcolac, which eats the sun and moon during eclipses.

A typical vampire of the reanimated-corpse type may have the attributes of a lover, as in Scott's William and Helen. The zmeu may also be such a lover.

The striga (pl. strigele) are not really vampires, but are sometimes confused with them. They are spirits either of living witches, which they send out as a little light, or of dead witches who can find no resting-place. These strigele come together in uneven numbers, seven or nine. They meet on rocky mountains, and dance and say:

"Nup, Cuisnup,
In casa cu ustoroi nu ma duc."
(I won't enter any house where there is garlic.)

They are seen as little points of light floating in the air. Their dances are exquisitely beautiful. Seven or nine lights start in a line, and then form into various figures, ending up in a circle. After they break off their dance, the may do mischief to human beings.

As regards the names used for vampires, dead and alive, strigoi (fem. Strigoica) is the most common Roumanian term, and moroii is perhaps the next most usual. Moroii is less often used alone than strigoi. Usually we have strigoi and moroii consorting together, but the moroii are subject to the strigoi. We find also strigoi, moroii, and varcolaci, and strigoi and pricolici used as if they were all were birds of the same feather. A Transylvanian term is siscoi. Varcolaci (svarcolaci) and pricolici are sometimes dead vampires, and sometimes animals which eat the moon. Oper is the Ruthenian word for dead vampire. In Bukovina, vidme is used for a witch; it covers much the same ground as strigoi (used for a live vampire), but it is never used for a dead vampire. Diavoloace, beings with two horns and spurs on their sides and feet, are much the same as vidme.

As Dr. Gaster reminds me, in many disenchantments we find phrases such as:

> *"De strigoaica, de strigoi,*
> *Si de case cu moroi,"*

[From vampires, male and female, and from a home with vampires,]

> *"De deochetori si de deochetoare,*
> *De moroi, cu moroaica,*
> *De strigoi cu strigoaica,"*

[From those who cast the evil eye (male or female), from vampires (male and female),]

> *"Ci, I dracul cu dracoaica, striga cu stigoiul,*
> *Deochiu cu deochitorul, pocitura cu pocitorul,*
> *Potca cu potcoiul,"*

[The devil with the female devil, the spirit of the dead witch with the vampire (male), the evil eye with the caster of the evil eye, the bewitchment with the bewitcher, the quarrel with the mischief maker.]

Ciuma, the plague, is occasionally one of the party. The strigoi and moroi are almost inseparable, hunting, however, with witches, wizards, and devils.

126

The nature spirits (ielele and dansele) have usually disenchantments of their own, for they work apart from vampires and Wizards, who are beings of human origin. While the peasant groups nature spirits apart from the more human workers of evil, he groups the living and the dead together, for the caster of the evil eye and the bewitcher are living men, though prospective vampires. The vampire, in fact, forms a convenient transition between human workers of evil and the devil, who resembles the dead vampire in not being alive in the flesh.

The vampire (a reanimated corpse) and the devil (a spirit) ought not, strictly speaking, to be alike, but the peasant, finding it difficult to imagine a spirit without a body, thinks of the devil in the form of a crow or a cat, or even in quasi-human form. The devil is a target for the thunderbolts of St. Elijah, and can be transfixed by one. Even the spirit of a living man, if separated from his body, must have some body or form. In Transilvania it is thought that many people can project their soul as a butterfly. In Valcea souls of vampires are considered to be incarnated in death's-dead moths, which when caught, should be impaled on a pin and stuck to a wall to prevent their flying further. A small, graceful thing which flutters in the air like a butterfly or a moth is as near as these peasants can get to the idea or pure spirit. The peasant in Siret goes a step further when he conceives of the soul as a little light. He has got beyond what is tangible.

The belief in vampires has often caused trouble to the rulers of Roumania. Ureche, in the *History of Roumania*, quotes the following:

"In 1801, on July the 12th, the Bishop of Siges sends a petition to the ruler of Wallachia, that he should order his rulers of provinces to permit no longer that the peasants of

Stroesi should dig up dead people, who had already been dug up twice under the idea that they were varcolaci" (term here used instead of strigoi).

In the *Biserica Orthodoxa Romana* (an 28) there is the following:

"The Arch bishop Nectarie (1813–19) sent round a circular to his higher clergy (protopopes) exhorting them to find out in what districts it was thought that the dead became vampires. If they came on a case of vampirism they were not to take it upon themselves to burn the corpse, but to teach the people how to proceed according to the written roll of the church."

The following accounts of vampires are taken from the Roumanian periodical of peasant art and literature, *Ion Creanga.* It was edited by my late friend, Tudor Pamfile, one of the most competent and industrious folklorists Roumania has ever had. The stories in *Ion Creanga* were taken down by careful observers, and published as nearly as possible in the exact words of the peasant.

N. I. Dumitrascu is responsible for the following, printed in *Ion Creanga* (volume 7, [1914], p. 165):

Some 20 or 30 years ago in the commune Afumati in Dolj, a certain peasant, *Marin Mirea Ociocioc*, died. It was noticed that his relations also died, one after the other. A certain *Badea Vrajitor* (Badea the Wizard) dug him up. Badea himself, going later into the forest, up to the frontier on a cold wintry night, was eaten by wolves. The bones of Marin were sprinkled with wine, a church service read over them, and replaced in the grave. From that time there were no more deaths in the family.

Some 15 years ago, in Amarasti, in the north of Dolj, an old woman, the mother of the peasant Dinu Gheorghita, died. After some months the children of her eldest son began to die, one after the other, and after that, the children of her youngest son. The sons became anxious, dug her up one night, cut her in two, and buried her again. Still the deaths did not cease. They dug her up a second time, and what did they see? The body whole without a wound. It was a great marvel. They took her and carried her into the forest, and put her under a great tree in a remote part of the forest. There they disemboweled her, took out her heart, from which blood was flowing, cut it in four, put it on hot cinders, and burnt it. They took the ashes and gave them to the children to drink with water. They threw the body on the fire, burnt it, and buried the ashes of the body. Then the deaths ceased.

Some 20 or 30 years ago, a crippled unmarried man, of Cusmir, in the south of Mehedinti, died. A little time after, his relations began to die, or to fall ill. This happened in several places. What could it be? "Perhaps it is the cripple; let us dig him up." They dug him up one Saturday night, and found him red as red, and all drawn up in a corner of the grave. They cut him open, and took the customary measures. They took out the heart and liver, burned them on red hot cinders, and gave the ashes to his sister and other relations, who were ill. They drank them with water, and regained their health.

In the Cusmir, another family began to show very frequent deaths, and suspicion fell on a certain old man, dead long ago. When they dug him up, they found him sitting up like a Turk, and red as red, just like fire, for had he not eaten up nearly the whole family of strong young men? When they tried to get him out he resisted, unclean and horrible. They gave him some blows with an ax, they got him out, but they could not cut him with a knife. They took a scythe and an ax, cut out his heart and liver, burnt them, and gave them to the sick folk to drink. They drank and regained their health. Then the old man was re-buried, and the deaths ceased.

In Vaguilesti, in Mehedinti, there was a peasant, Dumitriu
Vaideanu, of Transylvanian origin, who had married a
wife in Vaguilesti and settled there. His children died one
after the other, seven died within a few months of birth,
and some bigger children had died as well. People began to
wonder what the cause of all this could be. They took
counsel together, and resolved to take a white horse to the
cemetery one night and see if it would pass over all the
graves of the wife's relations. This they did, and the horse
jumped over all the graves, until it came to the grave of the
mother-in-law, Joanna Marta, who had been a witch,
renowned far and wide. Then the horse stood still, beating
the earth with its feet, neighing, and snorting, unable to
step over the grave. Probably there was something unholy
there. At night Dumitriu and his son took candles and went
to dig up the grave. They were seized with horror at what
they saw. There she was, sitting like a Turk, with long hair
falling over her face, with all her skin red, and fingernails
frightfully long. They got together brush-wood, shavings,
and bits of old crosses. They poured wine on her, they put in
straw, and set fire to the whole. Then they shoveled the
earth back and went home.

Slightly different methods are described by other observers
as employed in other districts:

In Romanati, the vampire was disinterred, undressed, and
put in a bag. The clothes were put back in the coffin, and
sprinkled with holy water, the coffin put back into the
grave, and the grave closed. A strong man carried the body
to the forest. The heart was cut out, the body cut up, and
one piece after another burnt. Last of all the heart was
burnt, and those present came near so that the smoke passed
over them, and protected them from evil. Here, as
elsewhere, is emphasized that the burning must be
complete. If the smallest piece of bone remains un-burnt,

the vampire can grow up again from it. In Zarnesti, when the vampire is dug up, iron forks are put into her heart, eyes, and breast, and she is re-buried with her face downwards.

In Mehedinti, it is sometimes considered sufficient to take the corpse far away to the mountains and leave it there. This is comparable with, but would not appear to be so efficient as, the Greek plan of taking the body of a vampire over the sea to an island.

The most general method for dealing with a vampire is as follows: it must be exhumed on a Saturday, as on all other days it will be wandered away from the grave. Either put a stake through the naval or take out the heart. The heart may be burnt on charcoal, or in a fire: it may be boiled, or cut into bits with a scythe. If the heart is burnt, the ashes must must be collected. Sometimes they are got rid of by throwing into a river, but usually they are mixed with water and given to sick people to drink. They may also be used to anoint children and animals as a means of warding off anything unclean. Sometimes however, the curse of a priest is sufficient to seal vampire in its tomb.

The tests to determine whether any dead man is a vampire, or not, are as follows:

*His household, his family and his livestock, and possibly even livestock of the whole village, died off rapidly.
*He comes back in the night and speaks with the family. He may eat what he finds in dishes and knock things about, or he may help with the housework and cut wood. Female vampires also come back to their children. There was a Hungarian vampire which could not be kept away, even by the priest and holy water.

*The priest reads a service at the grave. If the evil which is occurring does not cease, it is a bad sign.

*A hole about the size of a serpent may be found near the tombstone of a dead man. If so, it is a sign of the vampire, because vampires come out of graves by just such holes.

*Even in the daytime a white horse will not walk over the grave of vampire, but stands still and snorts and neighs.

*A gander, similarly, will not walk over the grave of a vampire.

*On exhuming the corpse, if it is a vampire it will be found to be:

(A) red in the face, even for months or years after burial.

(B) with the face turned downwards.

(C) with a foot retracted and forced into a corner of the grave or coffin.

(D) if relations have died, the mouth will be red with blood.

If the vampire is not recognized as such, and rendered innocuous, it goes on with its evil ways for seven years. First it destroys its relations, then it destroys men and animals in the village and in its country, next it passes into another country, or to where another language is spoken, and becomes a man again. He marries, and has children, and the children after they die all become vampires and eat the relations of their mother. This action of a vampire is probably suggested by the epidemics that would wipe out families and indeed villages in the countries of southeastern Europe. If, however we assume a vampire for every epidemic, they would certainly be only less plentiful than leaves of grass.

In case it is feared that any man may become a vampire, precautions must be taken at burial or soon after. As suicides are potential vampires, they should be dug up at once from their graves, and put into running water. A man may know that he was born with a caul, and leave word what is to be done to save his family from disaster. Or his relations may know of the danger and guard against it. There are various methods of avoiding this danger, and several may be used at the same time. The commonest method is to drive a stake through the heart or navel. In Valcea, it is sufficient to put a needle into the heart, but in Bulgaria it is a red hot iron which is driven through the heart. Small stones and incense should be put into the mouth, nose, ears, and navel, and under the fingernails, "so that the vampire may have something to gnaw." Garlic may also be placed in the mouth. Millet may be put in the coffin, or in the mouth and nose, so that the vampire will delay many days till it has eaten the millet. The body should be placed face downwards in the coffin. If it is a case of re-burial, the corpse should be turned head-to-foot.

The theory that New Englanders could have spontaneously developed so many methods for the destruction of the undead—organ-burning, ingestion of the ashes, and the less gruesome method of turning the corpse face-down—without direct contact to some branch of this folklore strains the possibilities of reason. Taken in consideration with the essentially foreign concept of vampirism itself, it becomes all but impossible to discount the likelihood of some catalytic event or presence in the early days of the American Colonies.

Chapter 12

Darker Shadows:
Yankee Vampires on the Silver Screen

Dark Shadows

Though lacking somewhat in vampires of a historical nature, Maine has become synonymous with tales of the fictional undead. At least two of horror's most infamous night stalkers call New England's largest state home. The first of these emerged from the unlikely storyline of an afternoon soap opera. Ask anyone old enough to remember the 1960s about the Gothic serial *Dark Shadows*, and I guarantee you will hear something like, "I used to run home from school every day to watch it!"

Set in the fictional Maine town of "Collinsport," *Dark Shadows* began its run in 1966 as a low-budget Gothic melodrama featuring a beleaguered governess and weekly sinister menaces. The show limped through its opening season with less than stellar ratings. By 1967, the show needed a serious boost to avoid cancellation. Series creator Dan Curtis opted for a make-or-break plot twist for the series—the introduction of an 18th-century vampire named Barnabas Collins.

The gamble paid off to a degree that exceeded anyone's wildest expectations. The popularity of the soap opera skyrocketed as America was swept up in *Dark Shadows* mania. The vampire Barnabas Collins soon was splashed all over magazines, trading cards, board games, and anywhere else his image could be stamped. The stumbling soap opera had become a media sensation, shattering traditional boundaries of daytime TV audiences. Over the next five years, the show would produce hit music, a series of novels, limitless tie-in merchandise, and a major motion picture.

The essential plot line of the early series concerned the arrival in Maine of a young governess, Victoria Winters. Employed by the wealthy and powerful Collins family, Victoria, an orphan, is in search of answers to her own identity. Following the introduction of Barnabas Collins, the central plot shifted to the vampire's attempts to rekindle his relationship with his 18th-century love Josette, now reincarnated in the body of a waitress named Maggie Evans. For those who lack the stamina to watch all of the 1,225 episodes of the original program, I highly recommend the cinematic film version called *House of Dark Shadows*, featuring most of the original cast, including Jonathan Frid as the vampire and Kathryn Leigh Scott as the heroine. The film provides an excellent condensed version of *Dark Shadow*'s most significant storyline—the resurrection of the vampire and his attempt to reclaim his reincarnated bride.

In 1992, the series was resurrected as an epic 12-episode miniseries, opening with the revival of the vampire Barnabas. The new script was adapted directly from the original 1960s series, though the character of Victoria Winters was the new object of the vampire's affection. Chock full of ghosts, witches, séances, and of course vampires, *Dark Shadows Resurrected* features well-known actor Ben Cross as Barnabas and Rhode Island–native Joanna Going as Victoria

Winters. Campy and over the top, the remake is still highly entertaining, a classic tale of love and revenge.

The 18th-century vampire Barnabas Collins
Photo courtesy of Dan Curtis Productions

The Newport, RI, mansion used for exteriors of "Collinwood" in the Gothic soap opera, *Dark Shadows*

'Salem's Lot

From prolific horror author Stephen King came the masterful 1975 novel *'Salem's Lot*. Salem's Lot is a fictional town near Portland, Maine, a sleepy New England town, brimming with unspoken secrets. The novel concerns the homecoming of modestly successful writer Ben Mears. His obsession with a childhood memory of something he witnessed in the local "haunted" house has called him home after many years to attempt to purge his fear of the hilltop mansion. Ben has concluded that the old building acts as a magnet for evil energies, drawing misfortune and death to the town. The hero's fears manifest more horribly than he could have predicted when the house becomes occupied by an ancient European vampire bent on a nihilistic quest to turn the entire town (and possibly beyond) into his undead minions.

The two television adaptations of King's novel (1979 and 2004) have both been high-quality efforts. The 1979 version, directed by genre veteran Tobe Hooper, is strangely divergent from the book in some areas (the master vampire, Barlow, has been reduced to a bald, snarling creature reminiscent of Max Schreck in the 1922 film *Nosferatu*), but stays mostly faithful to King's novel. Hooper's version does boast genuinely chilling, luminous-eyed vampires and a distinctly New England atmosphere. A poorly made sequel, *Return to Salem's Lot*, appeared on video several years after the first film, but is best avoided.

The 2004 remake updates the story in a variety of ways but keeps faithful to King's work for the majority of the story. The vampire Barlow is here played as a worldly charming gentleman, the "Mephistopheles" character of the tale who seduces and destroys the town one soul at a time.

'Salem's Lot is in many ways a contemporary reworking of *Dracula*. It features an arrogant aristocratic vampire, a desperate group of would-be vampire hunters, and nearly all

of the elements of the classic Gothic novel. King's vampire is a monstrously evil and debauched creature, reaching into his victims' souls and dredging up their darkest desires. King is at his best here, showcasing the most terrifying of evils—those that lurk beneath the surface of the human mind.

Let's Scare Jessica to Death

The final entry in our trilogy of on-screen Yankee vampires is the most true to the spirit of genuine New England folklore. Plagued by one of the worst film titles in cinema history, 1971s *Let's Scare Jessica to Death* has slipped into near obscurity in the decades since it was made. Staring a small cast of virtual unknowns, *Jessica* stands apart from the glut of modern horror/suspense films as a testament to style and subtlety. Although unarguably a vampire film, *Jessica* eschews cinematic vampire conventions, opting for an approach more reminiscent of a classic ghost story.

The script centers around the title character, a painfully insecure woman recently hospitalized for an apparent nervous breakdown. Sufficiently recovered, Jessica and her husband purchase a farmhouse in rural Connecticut (evoked eerily by the real Connecticut River Valley towns of Chester, East Haddam, and Old Saybrook). Along with a family friend, the couple relocates from New York to the farm in hopes of enjoying a less harried life. Arriving at the house they discover a girl, Emily, has been living in the empty house. Seeing an attraction between Emily and their friend, they allow the girl to stay. Soon after settling in, Jessica begins to experience a sense of unease about both Emily and the house. The discovery of an 18-century portrait resembling Emily, and a local legend of a girl who drowned in the cove behind the farm begin to weave an aura of dread, which is unsettlingly realized by the filmmakers. The vampire element is played with subtlety, and the overall effect of the film is that of a surreal nightmare.

Chapter 13

Medicine, Monsters, and Madness:
Scientific Theories on the Vampire Legend

Countless works of horror fiction have tried to lend a sense of respectability to their narrative with inventive pseudo-scientific rationales for the existence of the vampire. Authors such as Whitley Streiber and Colin Wilson have written about vampires resulting from parallel evolution, alien organisms, rare blood diseases, etc., making their tales of Gothic horror seem more plausible. Among these theories, the idea of a blood disease may come closest to touching on some truth. There are in existence a few unusual medical conditions to which science has recently connected the vampire legends.

One such disease is called Porphyria. Though Porphyria does *not* turn people into vampires, it can produce a number of symptoms that mimic characteristics of the stereotypical vampire. Aversion to the sun, blistering of the skin when exposed to sunlight, and in very rare instances a craving for blood may all manifest in the victim of Porphyria. The development of deformed teeth, pointed and sharp, or possibly stained red, are also among the effects that have been associated with the disease.

The connection between Porphyria and vampirism was first made in early 1985 by chemistry professor David Dolphin of the University of British Columbia. While addressing the American Association for the Advancement of Science, Dr. Dolphin theorized that people with Porphyria could find relief through the injection of heme, the blood component containing pigment. Dolphin contended that since a sufferer from Porphyria in earlier times would not have been able to *inject* heme into the bloodstream, the *ingestion* of large amounts of blood may have helped to alleviate the symptoms. Dr. Dolphin's theory has been widely disputed, but the similarities of symptom detailed in his research do provide a remarkable parallel to cinematic vampires.

A condition sometimes accompanying, and often associated with Porphyria, is Hypertrichosis, a genetic disorder that causes extreme and unnatural hair growth on the body. It was not unusual for a person with Hypertrichosis to be covered head to toe with hair, sometimes so thick it resembled fur. This may seem more suited to a werewolf than a vampire—and did indeed contribute to such beliefs—but folkloric vampires and werewolves shared a great number of traits, and in several countries it was believed that werewolves became vampires after death.

The one gap in Dr. Dolphin's theory seems to be the association of these conditions with the monsters of fiction, rather than those of folklore. While the vampires of Hollywood sport fangs and lily-white complexions, the undead of legend had no such features.

Tuberculosis, or "consumption" as it was commonly known, was the common thread in most of the cases of suspected vampirism in New England. The term tuberculosis applies to a group of related diseases of the upper respiratory system. It is characterized by breakdown of the tissue in the lungs. Shortness of breath, coughing—often accompanied by blood—and eventual wasting away of other vital functions occurs as progressively less oxygen reaches the blood. Through the 1800s, death was virtually certain for the victim of consumption, for no cure had yet been developed.

Interestingly, knowledge of tuberculosis did little to dissuade the people of Rhode Island and other New England states from assigning guilt to vampires. Those who became aware of the disease still assumed the carrier to be supernatural in origin. Apparently, the logic of tiny invisible animals carrying the malady from person to person was not much easier to swallow than the idea of vampires!

It is intriguing how superstition can be influenced by, and even grow from facts, sometimes resulting in folk remedies that actually do work. When a person is vaccinated against an illness, he or she is inoculated with an inactive or minor culture of that disease, to allow the body to build its defenses against that particular virus or germ. Perhaps the New England practice of ingesting the ashes from a suspected vampire started as an attempt on the part of some enterprising individual to create a "vampire vaccine."

Chapter 14

A Vampire of the Hills:
The New England Vampire in Verse

This atmospheric prose-poem from early 20th-century Imagist poet Amy Lowell eerily captures the spirit of a rural family confronted by the horror of vampiric possession. Ms. Lowell, a Massachusetts native, drew heavily on genuine accounts of regional vampires, several of which occurred in her lifetime.

A Dracula of the Hills
By Amy Lowell, 1926

Yes, I can understan' ther's a sort o' pleasure collectin' old
*   customs,*
An' linin' 'em up like a card o' butterflies.
Some of 'em's real quaint, I dare say,
But lookin's one thing an' livin's another.
Folks don't figger on th' quaintness o' th' things they're doin'.
'Ther' ain't no knick-knack about it then, I guess.
Times is changed since my young days,
Don't seem like th' same world I used to live in.
What with th' telephones an' th' automobiles,
An' city folks trampin' all over th' place Summers,
Lots o' things has kind o' faded out.

But I remember some queer goin's on.
They seem queer 'nough to me now, lookin' back.
We had good times a-plenty, nat'rally,
But they're all jumbled up together when I think on 'em,
I can't git ahold o' one more'n another,
While ther's some fearful strange things I can't never lose a
                mite of,
No matter how I try.
I'd like to forgit 'bout Florella Perry, but I ain't never be'n able to.
I don't know as you'd call it a custom.
'Twarn't th' first time th' like had happened, I know,
But ther' ain't never no such doin's nowadays.
Do the Lord's ways change, I wonder?
Superstition, you call it—but I don't know.
Seein's believin' all th' world over,
An' 'twas my own father seen it
An' others besides him.
I didn't, 'cause I was a young girl an' not let,
But I watched th' beginnin's;
An' what my eyes didn't see, my ears heerd,
An' that afore other folks' seein' was cold, as you might say.

'Twas all of forty year ago;
I was jest a slip of a girl drawn' toward th' beau stage but not
                yit ther'.
One day Id be thinkin' o' nothin' but ribbons,
An' th' next I'd go coastin' bellybumps all afternoon with
                th' boys.
Florella made me a woman for fair;
Maybe that was a good thing, 'twas time for it,
But I been a woman long 'nough now
An' I kind o' like to look back to what went afore.
I warn't livin' here then;
My husband was a Rockridge man
An' I come here when I married.

I was raised t'other side o' Bear Mountain to Penowasset.
Father kep' th' store ther'.
They thought a heap o' him in th' town
An' I had a happy childhood.
We didn't live over th' shop,
But quite along by th' end o' th' village
In a house my mother got from her father.
We had a couple o' fields an' a wood lot
An' kep' a hired man.
Father used to drive back an' forth in a buggy mornin's
            an' evenin's,
But mother an' me didn't miss for neighbors.
Jared Pierce owned a fine big farm just beyond us,
An' Joe Perry's was t'other side th' road.
Florella was Joe's wife,
An' a real pretty creature she was,
Fragile as a china plate
An' bright an' tidy as a June pink in sunshine.
She loved flowers;
Her door-yard was like a nosegay from May till October.
I never seen such flowers as hers;
Nobody else couldn't make 'em bloom so,
Even when she give 'em th' seeds.
Her snowdrops was always first up in th' Spring,
An' it took more'n a couple o' frosts to kill her late asters.
Th' way we knew she was ill was when th' garden begun to
            git weedy.
She an' Joe'd be'n married 'bout seven year then,
An' My! but they'd been happy!
Exceptin' for not havin' a child, I don't think ther' was a
            thing they wanted.

An' then Florella took sick.
It come with a cough one Winter,
An' she couldn't seem to git back her stren'th.

Come plantin' time, she couldn't do it.
Joe done his best, but that year th' garden warn't nothin'
      perticlar.
Florella used to set in her rocker on th' piazza lookin' at it
      an' cryin'.
Many's th' time I've slipped over an' done a little rakin'
      for her.
At first she liked me to do it,
But after a while she said to let it alone;
If it warn't her garden, she said, she didn't care nothin'
      'bout it.
She spoke almost fierce, I thought, an' I didn't go over agin
      for quite a spell.
When I did, Florella had took to her bed.
She was a queer kind of invalid. You couldn't seem to help her any.
She'd let you do things an' thank you,
But she always seemed angry that you had to come.
One day I was dustin' her room, an' she said to me:
"Becky, I ain't a-goin' to die."
"'Course you ain't, Florella," says I,
"Whatever put that into your head?"
She flared up at that.
"'Tain't no use lyin' to me, Becky Wales, I know I'm dyin'.
But I won't die. You'll see.
I'll find some way o' livin'.
Even if they bury me, I'll live.
You can't kill me I ain't th' kind to kill.
I'll live! I'll live, I tell
If ther's a Devil to help me do it!"
She screamed this out at me, settin' up in bed
An' pointin' with her finger.
I was so scared I had to grab a chair to keep from fallin',
An' Joe come runnin' in from th' barn.
He took her in his arms an' soothed her,
An' she bust out cryin' an' sunk into a little heap in th'
      big bed

148

So's you couldn't hardly see her, she was so thin.
Joe sent me home. He said not to mind Florella,
That she was flighty an' didn't know what she was sayin'.

Well, after that things got worse.
Florella had spell after spell;
You could hear her cryin' an' hollerin' way down th' road.
It was always th' same thing: she wouldn't die, nobody could
  make her die.
Twas awful pitiful to hear her takin' on.
Sometimes she'd moan an' moan,
An' then she'd break out crazy mad an' angry, screamin'
  for life.
Joe was at his wits' end.
Dr. Smilie said ther' warn't nothin' to do for her
'Cept give her quietin' draughts.
But Florella wouldn't take 'em;
She said they was a little death,
An' she'd throw down th' cup every time they give it to her.
Then she took a notion to see Anabel Flesche.
She was a queer sort of woman, was Anabel,
She lived in a little shed of a place over Chester way.
Some said she had Indian blood in her,
Anyway she was learn'd in herbs an' simples;
She claimed to know jest when to pick 'em,
An' she talked a lot o' foolishness about th' full o' th' moon,
An' three hours before dawn, an' th' dew o' th'
  second Friday,
An' things like that.
Well, Florella had her in,
An' she made her chamomile teas an' lotions, out o' leaves
  an' plants she'd gathered,
An' fussed around with bits o' wax an' string,
But Florella didn't change none. She kep' sinkin' an' sinkin',
An' th' cryin' spells got to comin' oftener.

She cried most o' th' time then.
I used to set in th' stair winder
When I'd oughter be'n in bed, listenin'.
It made my flesh creep to hear her poor cracked voice
            declarin' she wouldn't die,
An' all th' time she was dyin' plain as pikestaff.
I never see nobody so hungry for life;
She was jest starvin' for it.
Why, even when ther' warn't nothing' lef' of her but eyes
            an' bones,
She'd talk an' talk 'bout th' life she'd a right to, an' she was
            goin' to
have, come what or nothin'!
It was kind o' lonesome out our way then;
Most o' th' passin' got to go by th' Brook Road.
'Twarn't so handy by a good two mile,
But nobody couldn't a-bear to hear Florella callin' an' wailin'.
You couldn't count ten th' times she was still.
'Twas a awful witchin' sound, comin' through th' night th'
            way it did;
I know I got all frazzled out losin' my sleep for hearin' it.
Mother an' Mis' Pierce used to take it in turns to watch her,
An' 'twas a real kindness to do it, it wore th' nerves so.

One Saturday afternoon Mis' Pierce was with her,
When all of a suddint she jumped out o' bed,
Cryin' she was goin' int' th' garden,
That she was well now an' wouldn't be kep' back no more.
Mis' Pierce caught her just as she was goin' through th' door
An' ther' was a struggle, I guess.
Joe heerd where he was out in th' yard hoein' beans.
He was scared to death, an' jest heaved his hoe up onto
            his shoulder
An' run in as he was.
Florella seed him comin' with th' hoe up on his shoulder,
An' she screamed a fearful wild scream:

"You too, Joe!" she said,
"You want to kill me same as th' others?
But you shan't do it, I'll live to spite you, I'll live because
        o' you!"
She was mockin', an' grinnin', and' coughin',
An' menacin' him with her finger,
An' her head joggin' back an' forth from shoulder to
        shoulder like a rag-doll's.
Mis' Pierce run'd over an' tell'd Mother soon's she
        could git a minit, an' them was her very words.
Now Florella loved Joe as only a rare few women do love;
But she was jest plumb crazy by this time,
Worryin' 'bout th' life was leavin' her, an' all eat up
        with consumption.
But it didn't make no diff'rence to Joe,
He loved her always.
He jest picked her up an' laid her back in bed,
An' she went off unconscious an' never come to.
She died that night.
I mind it well, cause the' whippoorwills 'd been so loud
        th' night before;
When I'd heerd 'em. I'd thought Florella's time was come.

I've always hated funerals,
I can't a-bear to look on a corpse an' Florella's was dretful.
Not that she warn't pretty;
She was. Even her sickness hadn't spoiled her beauty.
She was like herself in a glass, somehow,
An old glass where you don't see real clear.
'Twas like music to look at her, only for her mouth.
Ther' was a queer, awful smile 'bout her mouth.
It made her look jeery, not a bit th' way Florella used to look.
If I shut my eyes I can see that face now,
Blue, an' thin, an' th' lips all twisted up an' froze so.
I guess I've seen that face in my mind every day for
        forty year, more or less.

Well, they buried her, an' we girls set pansies an'
      lobelia all about her grave
An' took turns tendin' 'em, week by week.
I'd loved Florella,
An', when she was dead, I rec'llected her as she was
'fore her sickness come, an' forgot th' rest.

Two years is a long time to watch a person die,
An' Joe'd done more nursin' than most husbands.
He kind o' pined when 'twas all finished,
But th' neighbors kep' a-droppin' in to see him,
An' Mother an' Mis' Pierce did him up every so often,
An' bye-n'bye he got ahold of himself,
An' seemed to be gittin' on nicely.
He was a proper good farmer, an' things was goin' well
      with him,
All ceptin' his sorrow, which nothin' couldn't lift, nat'rally,
When th' next Winter he caught a bad cold.
I guess he let it go too far afore he saw th' doctor;
Anyhow it got a good settle on him an' he couldn't shake
      it off.
Nobody'd have thought much of it, I guess, but for
Florella beginnin' th' same way.
Joe warn't concerned, he said he'd be all right come Spring,
But he warn't. He'd try to do his work as usual,
But soon he'd give over an' set down.
He was real patient, but he didn't git no better.
Dr. Smilie begun to look grave.

One day I went over with a bowl o' soup from Mother.
Joe was settin' in th' garden, by a bed o' portulaca;
They's cruel bright flowers, an' Joe looked so grey beside 'em
I got a start to see him.
"Becky," says he, "I know you loved Florella,
An' I should like you to have her flowers," says he.
"I've willed th' farm to my brother over to Hillsborough,

But you can dig up th' flowers afore he takes possession."
"Joe," I said, "Joe…" an' I couldn't get out another word for
          th' life o' me.
"Yes," he went on, "o' course I'm goin'. I've give her all I could,
          but it can't last.
Anabel Flesche was here yesterday, an' she told me.
I'm glad to ease her any, you know that, but it can't last."
Glad to ease Anabel Flesche—I thought,
But I know'd he didn't mean that.
I run right home an' told Mother, an' she told Father,
An' that evenin' they went down to Dr. Smilie's.
The doctor allowed 'twas consumption, but he was
          angry enough
'bout Anabel Flesche.
"I'll see that hussy stops her trapesin'," he said,
"Rilin' up a sick man with her witch stories," he said.
"I'll witch her, I'll run her out o' town if she comes agin!"
Anabel didn't come agin, but I guess she done it th' first time,
For Joe didn't seem to take int'rest in gittin' well.
When a man don't want to live, he don't live, an'
          that's gospel.
Joe went down hill so fast that by Midsummer ther' warn't
          no hope.
I used to set with him a good deal, an' 'twas queer how diff'rent he
          was to Florella.
I think he was th' quietest man I ever see.
He didn't seem to have no pleasure 'cept in speakin'
          'bout Florella.
By times he told me everythin':
How he courted her, an' what he said, an' th' way she looked when
he brought her home.
I got awful near life for a young girl with th' things he
          told me.
I've be'n married an' widowed since, but I don't know as I ever got
nearer to things than Joe's talk brought me.

153

Men ain't alike, an' women ain't alike, an' marriages is th'
    most unlike of all.
My marriage, when it come, was no more like Joe's
    an' Florella's
Than a piney's like a cabbage.
But this ain't my story.

"Florella had a strong will," says Joe to me one afternoon.
Autumn had come by then, an' some o' th' leaves had fell,
An' those that hung on were so bright they seemed to fairly
    smarten up th' sun.
Joe was layin' in his bed with a patchwork quilt over him,
A lovely one 'twas, the State House Steps pattern;
Florella'd made it, she was wonderful clever with her needle.
The' whole room was a blaze o' sunshine.
Right on the' chimbley hung a picture o' Florella.
Some travellin' artist had painted th' year she was married.
I don't suppose city folk would have made much of it.
But I thought 'twas a sweet pretty thing, an' th' spun-image
    o' Florella.
"Florella had a mighty strong will," says Joe agin.
"She owned me body an' soul, an' that was a rare pride
    to me."
I couldn't figger what to answer, so I didn't.
"I guess she owns me still, he says, an' I don't know if he was
    really talkin' to me.
"I'm glad she does. It's got to be both o' us, all or neither,
    together."
He smiled at that, very slow an' tired, almost as though it hurt
    his lips to do it.
"Perhaps you don't understand, little Becky," said he.
I don't know whether I did or not, an' I didn't have a chance
    to say,
For all of a sudden crash down come Florella's picture on th'
    floor with th' cord broke.
I jumped nearly out o' my skin, I expect I screamed too,

But Joe didn't so much as shiver.
"Yes," he said, lookin' at me with his steady smile,
"This proves it. You mark my words. It can't go on much longer.
Poor Florella!"
He sighed then an' layed down, an' I thought he went
  to sleep.
I picked up th' picture, but th' glass had cut it badly,
All about th' mouth too.
It made it look th' way Florella's corpse did an' give me
  a turn.
I was afeer'd Joe'd see it when he waked up, so I set it with its
  face aginst th' wall.
But I needn't have bothered, for Joe never waked up.
When Mother come, she didn't think he looked right,
An' she sent for Dr. Smilie.
He warn't dead when th' doctor got ther',
But he was unconscious an' hardly breathin';
He stayed like that for a day an' a night, an' then 'twas
  all over.
All over for Joe, yes, but not for us.

About a week after th' funeral, Father met Anabel Flesche.
"So Joe Perry's dead," whined Anabel, an' Father was
  sure th' old hag looked pleased.
He only said "Yes, he's dead," an' was pushin' on when Anabel
  stopped him.
"Florella's a determined woman," she cackled, "ain't
you afeerd she'll try somebody else?"
"What th' Hell do you mean?" cried out Father.
"She loved life," said Anabel, in a queer, sly way, "Joe's gone,
  but ther's others."
Father was so angry he couldn't trust himself to speak,
He jest touched up his horse an' drove on.
But what Anabel said rankled.
He an' Mother talked it over that night.
I warn't supposed to hear, but I did.

155

I was all shook up with th' things had happened
An' I daresn't stay in bed alone with nobody near,
So I used to creep out an' set on th' stairs 'till Father an'
Mother come up.
It comforted me to know they was in th' next room, an' I
        could sleep then.
Mother was real strict, an' I was always sent to bed at nine;
They'd come up 'bout ten, an' I'd set that hour on th' stairs
Where I could look int' th' kitchen an' see 'em.
That's how I come to hear.
Afterwards I allowed I knew, an' they told me everythin'.
Well, to make a long story short,
Father an' Jared Pierce went straight to th' Selectmen,
An told 'em what Anabel was hintin'.
Then some old people rec'llected things which had happened
        years ago,
An', puttin' two an' two together, they decided to see
        for themselves.
The Selectmen was all ther', an' Father, an' Jared Pierce;
They did it at night so's not to scare folks.
I warn't ther', but Father told it so I think I seen it:
Th' leaves blowin' an' sidlin' down,
Th' lantern light jerkin' 'long th' ground,
Th' noise o' th' pickaxes an' spades.
They got up th' coffin an' opened it.

Florella's body was all gone to dust,
Though 'twarnt' much more'n a year she'd be'n buried.
But her heart was as fresh as a livin' person's,
Father said it glittered like a garnet when they took th' lid off
        th' coffin.
It was so 'live, it seemed to beat almost.
Father said a light come from it so strong it made shadows,
Much heavier than th' lantern shadows an' runnin' in a
        diff'rent direction.

Oh, they burnt it; they always do in such cases, Nobody's safe
    till it's burnt.
Now, sir, will you tell me how such things used to be?
They don't happen now, seemingly, but this happened.
You can see Joe's grave over to Penowasset Buryin'ground,
    if you go that way.
The church-members wouldn't let Florella's ashes be put
    back in hers,
So you won't find that.
Only an open space with a maple in th' middle of it;
They planted th' tree so's no one wouldn't ever be buried in that
    spot again.

Chapter 15

A 19th-Century Perspective

The following article, published in the late 19th century, details the wide extent to which the New England vampire incidents became known in their day. It is believed to be the first published account of the Tillinghast Family vampire, as seen in chapter three. The author's opinion that these events were worthy of note is borne out by the survival of the article. It is especially significant in its allusions to other regional cases occurring at the time of publication.

The Belief in Vampires in Rhode Island

Sidney Rider, "Booknotes," March 1888

The belief in vampires — that is, in unseen beings, which though dead, nevertheless possess some attributes of a living existence — in beings which wander at night sucking the blood of living human victims — in bloodsucking ghosts, is a delusion of comparatively modern origin, at least in the form in which it will appear in the following narrative.

It appears to have had its origin in the lower Danubian provinces, in Servia, Bulgaria, Wallachia, Moldavia and the neighboring states. It doubtless developed from the earliest Greek mythology, for the Greeks believed there were beautiful phantom women who feasted themselves on the fresh blood of young men. Lamia was the name by which such beings were known in the Greek mythology.

As this legend traveled northward, it seems to have assumed a somewhat different character, and to have become more distinct or defined in form. An account of the superstition as it existed in 1679 was written by Rycaut, and published in his work on the "State of the Greek & Armenian Churches." These imaginary creatures about which we read in the "Arabian Nights" and which therein are styled ghouls, were believed to be possessed of the same characteristics as the vampire.

A vampire was developed from a human being who had died. During the day this unquiet spirit would lie quietly in the grave in which it was buried, but at night it would assume the form of some animal or insect, and wander forth, seeking and sucking the warm blood of its sleeping victim. There were believed to be methods of preventing a dead person from becoming a vampire, provided those methods were pursued before burial. In Eastern Europe, where this superstition originated, these methods were usually practiced.

At a later period another superstition, somewhat similar in form, arose in Western Europe. It was a belief in the Were-Wolf of Loup-Garou of the Norman French. Were-Wolf is an Anglo-Saxon word meaning, a man in the semblance of a wolf. This imaginary being was believed to assume the form of a wolf, or of a white dog, or of a black goat, and to wander forth at night devouring infants, and performing other like things. Its skin was proof against every missile other than a bullet which had been blessed at a shrine dedicated to Saint Hubert, the patron saint of huntsmen.

This form of the superstition appears never to have taken root in this country. The other form of the superstition seems to have been prevalent at one time here in Rhode Island. In fact, it may even at this day be held in her remote regions, if, indeed, that term be not inapplicable with the narrow confines of this little state. Strange, even incredible is it that anybody should believe in such absurd superstitions. It is true, nevertheless. There were, and there are now, those who do believe them, and the purpose of this paper is to narrate a case which took place here in Rhode Island at no very remote period. It was of a genuine vampire. Here, then, it is:

At the breaking out of the Revolution there dwelt in one of the remoter Rhode Island towns a young man whom we will call Stukeley. He married an excellent woman and settled down in life as a farmer. Industrious, prudent, thrifty, he accumulated a handsome property for a man in his station in life, and comparable to his surroundings. In his family he had likewise prospered, for Mrs. Stukeley meantime had not been idle, having presented her worthy spouse with fourteen children. Numerous and happy were the Stukeley family, and proud was the sire as he rode about the town on this excellent horses, and attired in his homespun jacket of butternut brown, a species of garment which he much affected. So much, indeed, did he affect it that a sobriquet was given him by the townspeople. It grew out of the brown color of his coats. Snuffy Stuke they called him, and by that name he lived, and by it died.

For many years all things worked well with Snuffy Stuke. His sons and daughters developed finely until some of them had reached the age of man or womanhood. The eldest was a comely daughter, Sarah. One night Snuffy Stuke dreamed a dream, which, when he remembered in the morning, gave him no end of worriment. He dreamed that he possessed a fine orchard, as in truth he did, and that exactly half the trees in it died. The occult meaning hidden in this revelation was beyond the comprehension of Snuffy Stuke, and that was what gave worry to him. Events, however, developed rapidly, and Snuffy Stuke was not kept long in suspense as to the meaning of his singular dream. Sarah, the eldest child, sickened, and her malady, developing into a quick consumption, hurried her into her grave. Sarah was laid away in the family burying ground, and quiet came again to the Stukeley family. But quiet came not to Stukeley. His apprehensions were not buried in the grave of Sarah.

His unquiet quiet was but of short duration, for soon a second daughter was taken ill precisely as Sarah had been, and as quickly was hurried to the grave. But in the second case there was one symptom or complaint of a startling character, and which was not present in the first case. This was the continual complaint that Sarah came every night and sat upon some portion of the body, causing great pain and misery. So it went on. One after another sickened and died until six were dead, and the seventh, a son, was taken ill. The mother also now complained of these nightly visits of Sarah. These same characteristics were present in every case after the first one. Consternation confronted the stricken household. Evidently something must be done, and that, too, right quickly, to save the remnant of this family.

A consultation was called with the most learned people, and it was resolved to exhume the bodies of the six dead children. Their hearts were then to be cut from their bodies and burned upon a rock in front of the house. The neighbors were called in to assist in the lugubrious enterprise. There were the Wilcoxes, the Reynoldses, the Whitfords, the Mooneys, the Gardners, and others. With pick and spade the graves were soon opened, and the six bodies brought to view. Five of these bodies were found to be far advanced in the stages of decomposition. These were the last of the children who had died. But the first, the body of Sarah, was found to be in a very remarkable condition. The eyes were opened and fixed. The hair and nails had grown, and the heart and the arteries were filled with fresh red blood. It was clear at once to these astonished people that the cause of their trouble lay there before them. All the

162

conditions of the vampire were present in the corpse of Sarah, the first that had died, and against whom all the others had so bitterly complained. So her heart was removed and carried to the designated rock, and there solemnly burned. This being done, the mutilated bodies were returned to their respective graves and covered. Peace then came to this afflicted family, but not, however, until a seventh victim had been demanded. Thus was the dream of Stukeley fulfilled. No longer did the nightly visits of Sarah afflict his wife, who soon regained her health. The seventh victim was a son, a promising young farmer, who had married and lived upon a farm adjoining. He was too far gone when the burning of Sarah's heart took place to recover.

The conditions here narrated are precisely similar to those alleged to have taken place in the Danubian provinces, and the remedy applied was the same. But in those countries certain religious rites were observed, and occasionally, instead of burning a part of the whole of a body, a nail was driven through the center of the forehead. At the period when this event took place, religious rites were things but little known to the actors in the scene, and fire in their hands was quite as effective an agent as an iron nail. Those from whom these facts were obtained little suspected the foreign character of the origin of the extraordinary circumstances which they described; but extraordinary as they are, there are nevertheless those still living who religiously believe in them.

The preceding paper was offered to the *Providence Journal*, and refused for the reason assigned, that it was sensational in character. The fatherly advice was given that I enlarge it and offer it to some sensational newspaper where it would doubtless find a market.

Regardless of the opinion of the *Journal*, I maintain that the tale which I have told deserves and will receive the consideration of thinking men. It details an extraordinary belief, considered in connection with the supposed enlightened intelligence of the American people. Since it was written, another similar case in Wakefield, Rhode Island, has come to my knowledge; and still another now is in contemplation in a family of respectable surroundings, several of the members of which have recently died. Such delusions ought to be obliterated, and the way to obliterate them is to expose them to the light of reason to educate men to better beliefs.

Following up on the legend of "Snuffy Stuke," Rhode Island historian Michael Bell was able to associate the legend with the family of Stukeley Tillinghast of Exeter, RI. Subsequent research by Mr. Bell provided a wealth of evidence to support the theory that Sarah Tillinghast, Stukely's deceased 19-year-old daughter had indeed been exhumed toward the end of the 18th century. Stukeley and his wife, Honor, appear to have had eleven children rather than fourteen at the time of Sarah's death, but this discrepancy is reasonably accounted for by the historical remoteness of the story. It is often the tendency of such tales to adopt romanticized devices such as prophetic dreams to heighten the drama upon retelling.

Afterword

The presence in New England of a strongly rooted vampire mythology is something of an enigma to folklorists. There is quite simply no other area in all of North America with such a wealth of vampire lore.

The specter of the undead preyed upon fears of the remote villages of New England for over a century. Some estimates claim that over a hundred incidents of "vampire" exhumation occurred. Most of these are lost to time, their tales having died with the families who suffered through them. A few such stories have survived however, pieced together from fragments by diligent folklorists and researchers—modern vampire hunters, on the trail of the most extraordinary true cases of their kind.

Folklorist Michael E. Bell theorizes that superstition found a fertile breeding ground in the rural New England communities of a century and a half ago. Tensions between the area's growing industrial movement, with its legacy of unhealthy environmental conditions, and the resistance to change and education found in the agricultural communities provided ample fuel for the festering of Old World fears. Newspapers of the day found the survival of vampire beliefs to be further proof of the ignorance of the farming people, and seized the opportunity to print scathing editorials on the subject. In the 1920s, well known New England horror author H. P. Lovecraft offered his own theory in *The Shunned House*, a chilling tale based on regional vampire stories. Lovecraft imagined an ancient family of vampires and warlocks who fled persecution in Europe, eventually coming to work for the Tillinghast family in Rhode Island!

With a constant stream of new cultural influences coming into the New England area through our major port cities, the wealth of tradition and myth here is no surprise. The vampire legend however, still seems so unique to the area that we are given to wonder at its source. We may never uncover exactly how this primarily Eastern European superstition came to settle here, or to have such a grip on our Yankee ancestors. There seems to be almost infinite room for exploration within the subject. Of the many cases alluded to in oral tradition, folktales, and various papers of the day, we have uncovered significant information on only a handful. Many more await our discovery, and if luck is with us we shall be digging up New England vampires for a long, long time.

Dark Century: A Vampire Timeline

This timeline attempts to lend a sense of context to the notable incidents of vampirism and vampire literature from the later eighteenth through the nineteenth centuries.

1776	Signing of American Declaration of Independence
1780	Spaulding family exhumations, Dummerston, VT
1789	George Washington elected president
1793	Rachel Burton exhumed, Manchester, VT
1796	Smallpox vaccine invented; Abigail Staples exhumed, Cumberland, RI
1799	Napoleaonic Wars begin; Sarah Tillinghast exhumed, Exeter, RI
1807	Anonymous vampire incident, Plymouth, MA
1819	Polidori publishes *The Vampire*
1827	Photography invented; Nancy Young exhumed, Foster, RI
1834	Mechanical harvester invented; Corwin family exhumations, Woodstock, VT
1847	Thomas P. Prest publishes *Varney the Vampyre*
1850	"J. B." vampire incident, Griswold, CT (approx. year)
1854	Henry Ray and sons exhumed, Jewett City, CT
1861	US Civil War begins
1870	15th Amendment allows African Americans to vote
1871	J. S. LeFanu publishes *Carmilla*
1874	Juliet Rose exhumed, Peacedale, RI
1876	Telephone invented
1889	Nellie Vaughn dies, West Greenwich, RI
1891	Trans-Siberian Railroad opened
1892	Mercy Brown exhumed, Exeter, RI
1893	Motion pictures invented
1896	Publication of Stetson's "Animistic Vampire in New England" and "Vampires in New England" in the *New York World*
1897	Bram Stroker publishes *Dracula*

Selected Bibliography and Suggested Reading

BOOKS

Barber, Paul, *Vampires, Burial and Death*, 1988. Yale University Press.

Bell, Michael E., *Food for the Dead*, 2001. Carrol & Graf.

Bowditch, Henry, *Consumption in New England*, 1862. Ticknor & Fields.

Citro, Joe, *Passing Strange*, 1996. Chapters Publishers.

Dresser, Norine, *American Vampires*, 1989. New River Press.

Eno, Paul, *Faces at the Window*, 1998. New River Press.

Florescu, Radu, and Raymond McNally, *In Search of Dracula*, 1972. Warner Books.

Melton, J. Gordon, *The Vampire Book*, 1994. Visible Ink Press.

Norris, Curt, *Ghosts I Have Known*, 1998. Covered Bridge Press.

PERIODICALS

Clauson, James Earl, "These Plantations," December 23, 1936. *Providence Journal Bulletin*.

Deveau, Mary Rose, "A Vampire in Griswold?", 1994. *Independent*.

Hamenway, Abby, *Vermont Historical Gazetteer*, Vol. V, circa 1875.

SUGGESTED READING

'Salem's Lot, by Stephen King. See Chapter 12 of this fictional vampire masterwork.

Dark Shadows — Angelique's Descent, by Lara Parker. An original novel based on the *Dark Shadows* television series.

Bloodlines, edited by Lawrence Schimel and Martin H. Greenberg. American Vampire Series, Cumberland House. A collection of classic and original short stories.

Appendix

Notes on Prologue
1. Foster's Observations During a Voyage Around the World.
2. Primitive Culture.
3. Cited from Götze's Russ., Volkls., p 62.
4. Cited by Calmet.
5. Tablet K 162, in British Museum.
6. Cited by Calmet.
7. Rhode Island has the largest population to the square mile of any state in the Union. The town of Exeter, before mentioned, incorporated in 1742–43, had but 17 persons to the square mile in 1890, and in 1893 had 63 abandoned farms, or one-fifth of the whole number within its limits. Foster, incorporated in 1781 and taken from Scituate (which was settled by Massachusetts emigrants in 1710), had in 1890 a population of 1,252, and in 1893 had eight abandoned farms, Scituate having fifty-five. North Kingston had 76 persons to the square mile in 1890. Mr. Arnold, in his history of the state, says, "South Kingston was in 1780 by far the wealthiest town in the State." It had a special provision made for the "maintenance of religion and education."
8. *Teutonic Mythology*.

Notes on Chapter 6
Literature Cited:

* Aries P (1981) *The Hour of Our Death*. New York: Alfred A. Knopf.
* Barber P (1988) *Vampires, Burial and Death: Folklore and Reality*. New Haven, CT: Yale University Press.
* Brown L (1941) *The Story of Clinical Pulmonary Tuberculosis*. Baltimore, MD: Williams and Wilkins Co.
* Cahill RE (1989) *New England's Things That Go Bump in the Night*. Peabody, MA: Chandler-Smith Publishing.
* Clark GA, Kelley MA, Grange JM, and Hill MC (1987) The evolution of microbacterial disease in human populations. *Current Anthropology* 28:45–51.
* Clausen JE (1936) These Plantations. *Providence Evening Bulletin*, December 23, 1936.
* Clausen JE (1937) *These Plantations*. Providence, RI: Roger Williams Press, EA Johnson Company.
* Dresser N (1989) *American Vampires: Fans, Victims, and Practitioners*. New York: Vintage Books/Random House.
* Exhumed the Bodies/Testing a Horrible Superstition in the Town of Exeter/Bodies of Dead Relatives Taken from their Graves. *Providence Journal*, March 19, 1892, p. 3.
* Hawke DF (1988) *Everyday Life in Early America*. New York: Harper & Row.
* Kelley MA, and Eisenberg LE (1987) Bastomycosis and tuberculosis in early American Indians: A biocultural view. *Midcont. J. Archeol.* 12:89–116.

* Kelley MA, and Micozzi MS (1984) Rib lesions and chronic pulmonary tuberculosis. *Am J Phys Anthropol.* 65:381–386.
* Kinder N (1971) The "Vampires" of Rhode Island. In AN Stevens (ed), *Mysterious New England.* Dublic, NH: Yankee Publishing.
* Mann RW, and Murphy SP (1990) *Regional Atlas of Bone Disease: A Guide to Pathologic and Normal Variation in the Human Skeleton.* Springfield, IL: Charles C. Thomas.
* Mann RW, Bass WM, and Meadows L (1990) Time since death and decomposition of the human body: Variables and observation in case and experimental field studies. *J Forens Sci.* 35:103–111.
* Mansfield DL (1884) *The History of the Town of Dummerston.* Ludlow, VT: A.M. Hemenway.
* McCully RS (1964) Vampirism: Historical perspective and underlying process to a case of autovampirism. *J. Nerv. Mental Dis.* 193:440–452.
* McFarland G (1990) *The "Counterfeit" Man: The True Story of the Boorn-Colvin Murder Case.* New York: Pantheon.
* Micozzi MS (1992) *Postmortem Change in Human and Animal Remains: A Systematic Approach.* Springfield, IL: Charles C. Thomas.
* Owsley DW (1990) The skeletal biology of North American historical populations. In JE Buikstra (ed.), *A Life in Science: Papers in Honor of J. Lawrence Angel.* Center for American Archeology, Kampsville, IL Scientific Papers #6, pp. 171–190.
* Perkowski JL (1989) *The Darkling: A Treatise on Slavic Vampirism.* Columbus, OH: Slavica Publishers.
* Phillips D (1929) *Griswold—A History: Being a History of the Town of Griswold Connecticut from the Earliest Times into the World War in 1917.* Reproduction by Unigraphics, Inc., Evansville, Indiana, 1977. Tuttle, Morehouse, and Taylor, p. 135.
* Prins H (1984) Vampirism: Legendary or clinical phenomenon? *Med. Sci. Law* 24:283–293.
* Prins H (1985) Vampirism: a clinical condition. *Br. J. Psych.* 146:666–668.
* Simister FP (1978) *A Short History of Exeter, Rhode Island.* Exeter Bicentennial Commission.
* Sledzik PS and Moore-Jansen PH (1991) Dental disease in nineteenth century military skeletal samples. In MA Kelley and CS Larsen (eds.), *Advances in Dental Anthropology.* New York: Wiley-Liss, pp. 215-224.
* Stephens R (1970) The vampire's heart. In WR Hard and JC Greene (eds.), *Mischief in the Mountains.* Montpelier, VT: Vermont Life Magazine Press, pp. 71–80.
* Stetson G (1898) The animistic vampire in New England. *Am. Anthropol.* 9:1–13.
* Stoker B (1983) *Dracula.* New York: Oxford University Press.
* Superstitions of New England. *Old Colony Memorial and Plymouth County Advertiser*, May 4, 1822, page 4.
* Vanden Bergh RL, and Kelly JF (1964) Vampirism: a review with new observations. *Arch. Gen. Psych.* 11:543–547.
* Wright D (1973) *The Book of Vampires.* New York: Causeway Books.